MW01471205

MICROWAVE
Snacks & Desserts

Tarla Dalal
India's #1 Cookery Author

S&C
SANJAY & CO.
MUMBAI

Other Books By Tarla Dalal

INDIAN COOKING
- Tava Cooking
- Rotis & Subzis
- Desi Khana
- The Complete Gujarati Cook Book
- Mithai
- Chaat
- Achaar aur Parathe
- The Rajasthani Cookbook
- Swadisht Subzian
- Punjabi Khana
- Mughlai Khana
- South Indian Recipes [New]

TOTAL HEALTH
- Low Calorie Healthy Cooking [New]
- Pregnancy Cookbook
- Baby and Toddler Cookbook
- Cooking with 1 Teaspoon of Oil
- Home Remedies
- Delicious Diabetic Recipes
- Fast Foods Made Healthy
- Healthy Soups & Salads
- Healthy Breakfast
- Calcium Rich Recipes
- Healthy Heart Cook Book
- Forever Young Diet
- Healthy Snacks
- Iron Rich Recipes
- Healthy Juices
- Low Cholesterol Recipes
- Good Food for Diabetes
- Healthy Subzis
- Healthy Snacks for Kids

WESTERN COOKING
- The Complete Italian Cookbook
- The Chocolate Cookbook
- Eggless Desserts
- Mocktails & Snacks
- Thai Cooking
- Soups & Salads
- Mexican Cooking
- Chinese Cooking
- Easy Chinese Cooking
- Sizzlers & Barbeques
- Cakes & Pastries
- Party Drinks [New]
- Wraps & Rolls [New]

- High Blood Pressure Cook Book
- Low Calorie Sweets
- Nutritious Recipes for Pregnancy
- Diabetic Snacks
- Zero Oil Rotis & Subzis
- Zero Oil Soups, Salads & Snacks
- Zero Oil Dal & Chawal
- Acidity Cook Book
- Growing Kids Cookbook
- Soya Rotis & Subzis
- Cooking with Sprouts
- Exotic Diabetic Cooking - Part 1
- Healthy Diabetic Cooking
- Protein Rich Recipes
- Eat Well Stay Well [New]
- Weight Loss after Pregnancy [New]
- 100 Calorie Snacks [New]
- Top 10 Healthy Foods [New]
- Healthy Starters [New]

MINI SERIES
- Cooking Under 10 minutes
- Pizzas and Pasta
- Fun Food for Children
- Roz ka Khana
- Idlis & Dosas
- Microwave - Desi Khana
- Paneer
- Parathas
- Chawal
- Dals
- Sandwiches
- Quick Cooking
- Curries & Kadhis
- Chinese Recipes
- Jain Desi Khana
- 7 Dinner Menus
- Jain International Recipes
- Punjabi Subzis
- Chips & Dips

- Corn
- Microwave Subzis
- Baked Dishes
- Stir-Fry
- Potatoes
- Recipes Using Leftovers
- Noodles
- Lebenese
- Cook Book for Two's
- Know your Dals & Pulses
- Fruit & Vegetable Carving
- Know your Spices
- Know your Flours
- Popular Restaurant Gravies
- Know Your Green Leafy Vegetables [New]
- Paneer Snacks [New]
- Pressure Cooker Recipes [New]
- Faraal Foods for Fasting Days [New]
- Finger Foods for Kids [New]

GENERAL COOKING
- Exciting Vegetarian Cooking
- Microwave Recipes
- Saatvik Khana
- The Pleasures of Vegetarian Cooking
- The Delights of Vegetarian Cooking
- The Joys of Vegetarian Cooking
- Cooking with Kids
- Snacks Under 10 Minutes
- Ice-Cream & Frozen Desserts
- Desserts Under 10 Minutes
- Entertaining
- Microwave Snacks & Desserts
- Kebabs & Tikkis
- Non-fried Snacks
- Mumbai's Roadside Snacks [New]
- Tiffin Treats for Kids [New]

Fourth Printing : 2010

ISBN : 978-8-186469-96-5

Copyright © Sanjay & Co.

Price Rs. 250/-

Published & Distributed by :
SANJAY & COMPANY
A-1/353, Shah & Nahar Industrial Estate, Dhanraj Mill Compound,
Lower Parel (W), Mumbai - 400 013. INDIA. Tel. : (91-22) 4345 2400.
Fax : (91-22) 2496 5876 • E-mail : sanjay@tarladalal.com • Website : tarladalal.com

"Tarla Dalal" is also a registered trademark owned by Sanjay & Co.

ALL RIGHTS RESERVED WITH THE PUBLISHERS.
No portion of this book shall be reproduced, stored in retrieval system or transmitted by any means, electronic, mechanical, photocopying, recording or otherwise, without the written permission of the publishers.

Disclaimer : While every precaution has been taken in the preparation of this book, the publishers and the author assume no responsibility for errors or omissions. Neither is any liability assumed for damages resulting from the use of information contained herein.

BULK PURCHASES : Tarla Dalal Cookbooks are ideal gifts. If you are interested in buying more than 500 assorted copies of Tarla Dalal Cookbooks at special prices, please contact us at 91-22-4345 2400 or email : sanjay@tarladalal.com

---

UK and USA customers can call us on :
UK : 02080029533   •   USA : 213-634-1406
For books, Membership on **tarladalal.com**, Subscription for **Cooking & More** and Recipe queries
Timing : 9.30 a.m. to 7.00 p.m. (IST), from Monday to Saturday
Local call charges applicable

Recipe Research & Production Design	**Copy Editor**	**Food Styling**	**Design**	**Printed by :**
Pinky Chandan Dixit Pradnya Sundararaj Arati Fedane	Nisha Katira	Pinky Chandan Dixit Pradnya Sundararaj	Satyamangal Rege	Minal Sales Agencies, Mumbai.
	Photography Vinay Mahidhar Jignesh Jhaveri (Double Spread & Page nos. 59,89)			**Typesetting** Adityas Enterprises

INTRODUCTION

Like most microwave users you probably only use your microwave for re-heating coffee or leftover dinner. My book "Microwave Snacks and Desserts" shows you the true potential of the amazing microwave in your kitchen.

All your favourite dishes can be cooked in the microwave with a minimal fuss. You'd be surprised how quickly the snacks and desserts can be prepared and you can cook and serve in the same dish too, so there's less washing.

I have gathered together recipes that will inspire you to use your microwave to the fullest. There are sections on starters and snacks, tea time treats and breakfast... all of which can be prepared in a jiffy at the press of a button. Your tiny tots will love the recipes in Children's Favourite section. And here, unlike on the stove, your little ones can actually help you as it is a lot cleaner and safer cooking with a microwave.

And for a sweet finale there's a spread of **Indian and Continental Desserts**. Time consuming recipes like **Shahi Rabdi, Bread and Butter Pudding** can be whipped up with grace and ease.

All the recipes are tried and perfected in a 20 litre, 900 watt microwave oven. The cooking time for the recipes may differ slightly, depending upon the size and wattage of your microwave oven.

Try all of these recipes in your trusted microwave...the wonder appliance. No more slaving for hours over the stove; simply sit back and enjoy home cooked Snacks and Desserts with your family and friends.

Cheers,

Tarla Dalal

ABOUT MICROWAVE OVENS

The microwave oven has revolutionized the way we cook. Not only does food cook quickly, one can cook and serve in the same dish, thus minimizing clean up time. Microwave cooking also tends to be low fat and hence is good for calorie watchers. Vegetables cook wonderfully, steamed to crisp-tender, remaining bright and fresh tasting, while retaining all their vitamins and nutrients.

Food cooks evenly, quickly and efficiently in the microwave. The nutrients are preserved, so the actual taste of the food is retained to a higher degree. Only a minimum amount of oil is required for cooking Continental as well as traditional Indian dishes so it seems desirable from the health point of view.

Also shorter and controlled cooking time means that the food does not get burnt or over-cooked. Another major advantage is that food is cooked minus the smoke, grease and heat and so your kitchen is always mess free and ready to welcome guests.

Microwaves provide a host of new shortcuts and problem solvers for chores such as roasting papads, blanching vegetables, making popcorn, idlis and dhoklas. Soggy and soft namkeens and nuts crispen on microwaving for only a minute, but that is only a part of its value. If you're using your microwave solely for these types of chores, you're not taking full advantage of its potential.

Many dishes that traditionally require constant stirring, such as sauces, halwas, gravies, besan laddu, chunda etc. can be made in the microwave in minutes with very little attention. You can also use the microwave to partially pre-cook foods that generally taste better cooked conventionally, like baked potatoes, and still cut the cooking time by half. Little wonder then, that microwave ovens have now earned a place in thousands of Indian homes.

TYPES OF MICROWAVE OVENS

I am often asked which oven is the best to buy…whether conventional or a simple microwave oven. There are many factors to consider when making a choice…

- Your needs..i.e do you need it only to reheat and cook or will you be dabbling with baking and grilling as well.
- Space available in your kitchen.
- Your budget.

You can choose from a wide variety of products that are easily available depending on your preference and your budget. There are imported brands and then there are numerous local brands available that are quite as good and are also more reasonable. There are 2 basic types of microwaves available in the market today.

1. **Simple microwave ovens :**

   These type of a microwaves work on the principle of radiation where the water molecules on the food get heated up which in turn causes the food to cook faster without the loss of nutrients. It can be used to cook, heat, re-heat, defrost etc. The only disadvantage is that foods cooked in this type do not get browned or coloured.

2. **Microwave and convection ovens :**

   These combine the speed of a simple microwave with the browning and baking of conventional ovens. They can be used as a regular oven as well as a microwave oven. With this function, one is able to cook food quickly using microwave option at the same time, the food can be browned and also crisped, using the oven/grill option. These are both features that regular microwave ovens cannot do. You can also use the microwave and grill/oven option in unison for quick and effective cooking. One should use vessels that are suitable for microwave and convection for e.g pyrex, borosil; etc. if using the combination method.

HOW EXACTLY DOES THIS MAGIC BOX WORK?

Microwaves act in three different ways.

Absorption - When the food is microwaved, the water molecules present in the food get stimulated and heated up, so the energy of the microwave is concentrated on cooking the food faster.

Transmission - Microwaves are attached only to water molecules and so they ignore everything else except the food to be cooked.

Reflection - Microwaves are absorbed by food and pass through materials like glass, china, wood, paper and plastic, but they reflect on metal.
When metallic objects are placed in a microwave oven, the energy pattern becomes disrupted and distorted due to reflection. This condition produces arcing. Arcing is a reaction that occurs when you place metal dishes in the microwave. It causes small sparks in the oven as a result of friction between the rays and metal. This is called arcing.

CHOOSING MICROWAVE COOKWARE

The markets are flooded with many different types of cooking utensils that are microwave safe. Plastics, paper, glass, ceramic etc. all claim to be microwave safe and friendly. Plastic and paper are good for short term cooking or re-heating only. Avoid using unbranded plastic products in the microwave as they can emit harmful chemicals into your food. Corning ware, glass and ceramics are thus a better option.

TEST A DISH FOR MICROWAVE SAFETY

Before using any utensil for the first time, carry out this simple test to ascertain whether it is microwave safe. Fill the vessel with approximately 200 ml of water and microwave on HIGH for 2 minutes. If the utensil gets too warm, it should not be used. The water should get heated without heating the vessel.

Listed below is the cookware, which can be used for the microwaves and that which should be avoided.

Cookware which can be used	Cookware to be avoided
Oven proof chinaware, glass (Borosil, Arcorac etc) and pottery dishes.	Plastics and melamine cannot withstand the heat emitted by microwaves, hence should be avoided for prolonged use.
Ceramic dishes can be used provided they are non-porous. To check if the dish is non-porous, heat it in the microwave for 15 to 20 seconds. The dish should not feel warm.	Dishes with a sloping base causes the food in the shallow parts to get over heated and prevents even cooking of the food.
Paper plates, towels and 100 % cotton and linen napkins can be used only for re-heating and not for cooking.	Metal dishes and foil should not be used while cooking in a microwave.
Wood items can be used in the micro-oven but only for short cooking periods.	Cookware with golden, silver or metal rims as this may cause arcing.
Loose-fitting or micro-safe lids, cling-wrap, but with a few holes made in it to allow steam to escape.	Tight fitting lids, foil and metal lids.
Shallow and straight dishes work better than deep ones as they ensure faster and uniform cooking.	Deep bowls, in which food gets unevenly distributed and so unevenly cooked.

SAFETY FEATURES....DO'S AND DON'TS

- The microwave oven door should not be subject to any strain.
- It should not be used often and also a bang is to be avoided. Any misalignment may cause leakage of the microwave.
- Small quantities of food with low moisture content can burn, spark or catch fire if re-heated for long.

- Do not operate an empty oven as it can cause damage to the oven.
- Keep at least five cms space between the back of the oven and the wall immediately near it as it allows the exhaust air to escape.
- Do not install the oven near gas burners or near radios or TVs.
- Do not deep fry in the oven as it is not possible to control the temperature of the oil and it may result in catching fire easily.
- If food catches fire turn off the oven and remove the plug out but do not open oven door.
- Keep the interior of the oven clean as small specks of food particles inside can reduce its efficiency.
- Do not cook eggs with the shells as they explode.
- Do not heat food or liquids in bottles with lids closed.
- Pierce vegetables and fruits with tight skin to prevent them from bursting before cooking them.
- Dishes must be ½ or ¾ filled depending on the liquid content of the food. If the dish is too small, the food will boil over and if the dish is too large the thick curry will spread out and overcook.

LOOKING AFTER YOUR MICROWAVE

- Always wipe the microwave with a damp cloth after use but remember to disconnect from electric supply before cleaning.
- Do not use abrasive cleaners, knives etc. as they may cause scratches.
- If the oven cavity starts smelling, keep a container with lime water or a solution of vanilla essence and water and heat it to a boiling point.
- Removable shelves and racks should be washed with warm water and wiped dry before being re-used.
- The microwave should never be used empty, without any food in it, as this could cause damage.

1. PANHA, Recipe on page 98
2. POHA CHIVDA, Recipe on page 35
3. MASALA PEANUTS, Recipe on page 38
4. SOYA CRISPS, Recipe on page 40

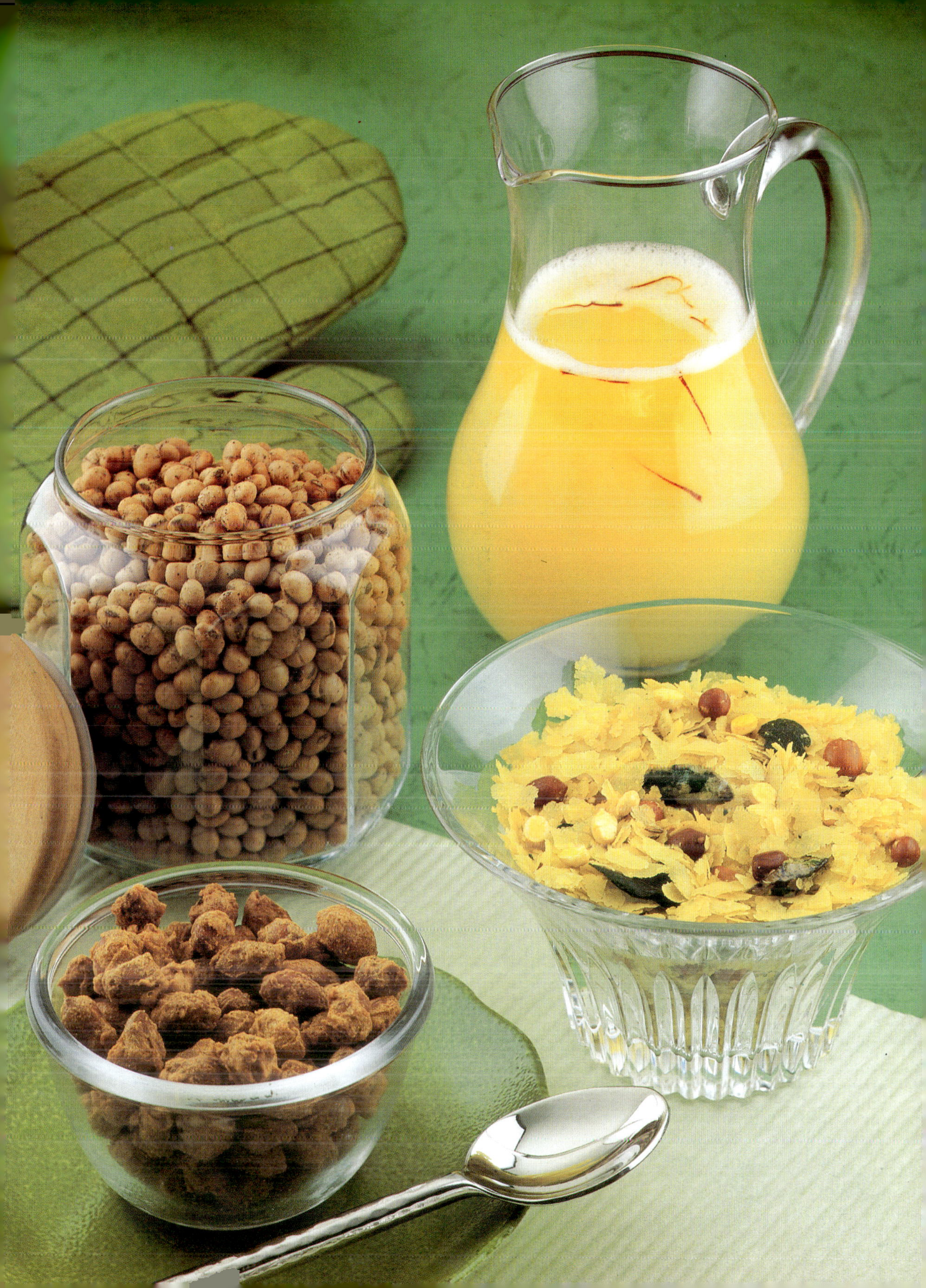

INDEX

BREAKFAST

Poha Khichu	16
Batata Poha	17
Seviyan Upma	18
Upma	22
Rawa Idli	23
Green Peas Dhokla	25
Palak Methi Dhokla	26
Panki	27
Orange Marmalade	29
Apple Jam	30
Strawberry Jam	30
Makai Sheera	32
Jowar Khichu	33

TEA-TIME TREATS

Poha Chivda	35
Papad Poha	36
Baked Papdi	37
Masala Peanuts	38
Cinnamon Crisps	39
Soya Crisps	40
Besan Laddoo	41
Jeera Kand Wafers	42
Low Cal Potato Wafers	43
Banana Pepper Wafers	44
Soya Namak Paras	45
Cheesy Cornflakes	46

DIPS AND DRINKS

Chunky Broccoli and Corn Dip 92
Baba Ghanouj 93
Bengali Tomato Chutney 94
Barbeque Dip 95
Creamy Cheese Dip 96
Kokum Sherbet 97
Panha 98
Saunf Sherbet 99

INDIAN DESSERTS

Pineapple Kesari 101
Shahi Rabdi 102
Rice Kheer 103
Coconut Barfi 104
Doodhi Kheer 105
Walnut Barfi 106
Apple Kheer 108
Bhappa Doi 109
Makai Jajaria 110
Garam Golpapdi 111

CONTINENTAL DESSERT

Chocolate Sponge Cake 113
Vanilla Sponge Cake 113
Chocolate Brownie 114
Double Layered Chocolate Truffle Gateau 116
White Chocolate Fudge 119
Dark Chocolate and Peanut Butter Bites 120
Bread and Butter Pudding 121

Breakfast

6. Add the lemon juice and mix well.
   Serve hot garnished with the grated coconut and chopped coriander.

Handy tip : *If the poha gets too dry sprinkle a tablespoon of milk, mix well and serve immediately.*

SEVIYAN UPMA

Seviyan make an interesting alternative to the regular semolina for making upma. This recipe works well using rice noodles too!!

Preparation time : 10 minutes.   Cooking time : 7½ minutes.   Serves 4.

1 cup vermicelli (seviyan)
1 teaspoon mustard seeds (rai)
1 teaspoon urad dal (split black lentils)
¼ teaspoon asafoetida (hing)
1 teaspoon chopped ginger
1 to 2 green chillies, slit
3 to 4 curry leaves
½ cup onions, chopped
¼ cup coriander leaves, chopped
1 teaspoon oil
salt to taste

To serve
lemon wedges

1. Heat 2 cups of water with some salt and 1 teaspoon oil in a microwave safe bowl and microwave on HIGH for 2 minutes. Add the vermicelli and keep aside for 5 minutes or till the vermicelli is cooked.
2. Drain out any excess water and keep aside.
3. In another microwave safe bowl, combine the oil, mustard seeds, urad dal and asafoetida and microwave for 2 minutes.
4. Add the curry leaves and ginger and chillies and microwave for ½ a minute.
5. Add the onions and microwave on HIGH for another 2 minutes.
6. Add the vermicelli, coriander and salt and mix well.
7. Microwave on HIGH for 1 minute and serve with lemon wedges.

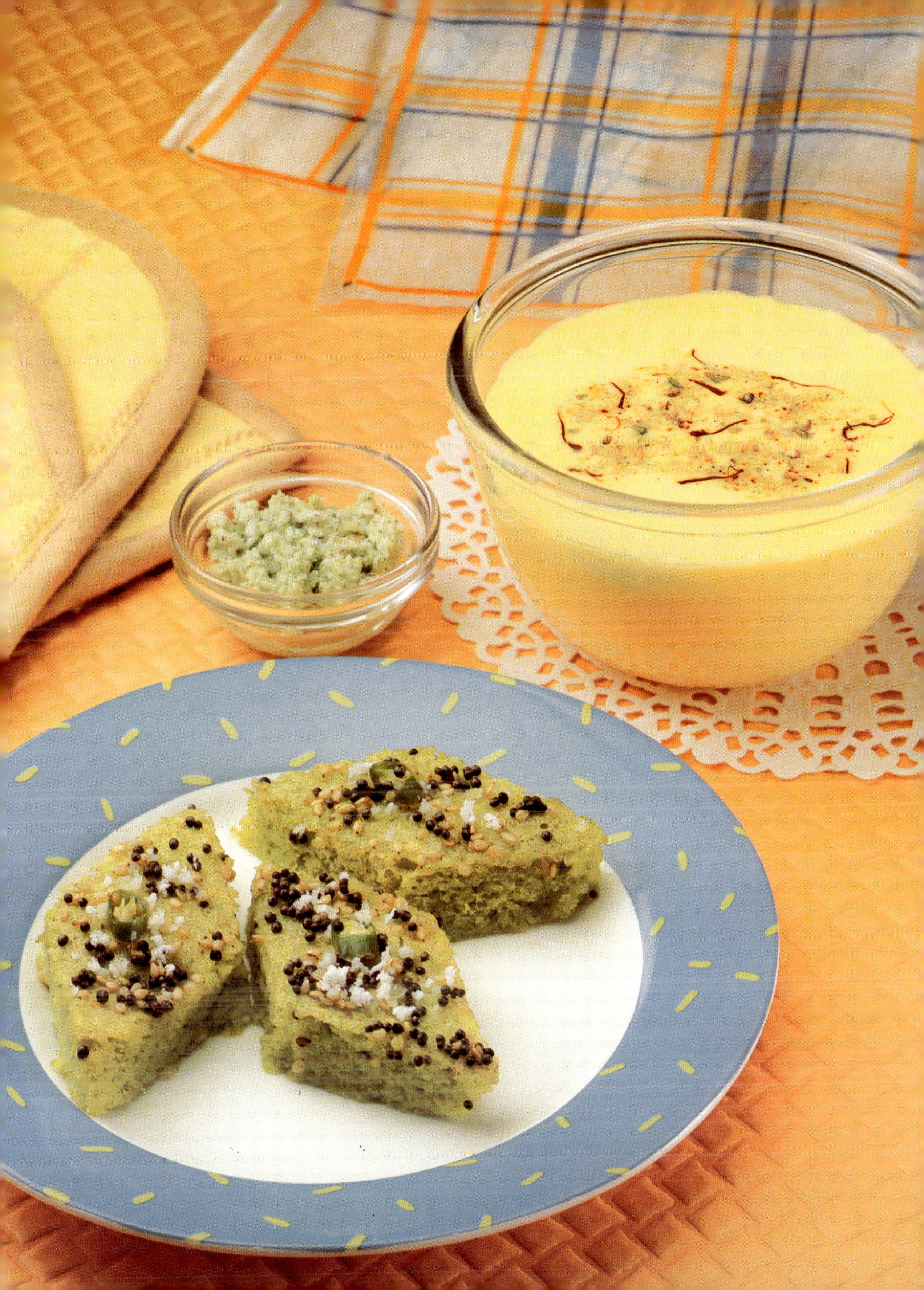

UPMA

You no longer need to sweat over roasting rawa to make upma. Serve it with a dash of lemon to add zing to your breakfast.

Preparation time : 5 minutes.   Cooking time : 10 minutes.   Serves 4.

½ cup rawa (semolina)
½ teaspoon mustard seeds (rai)
½ teaspoon urad dal (split black lentils)
½ cup onions, finely chopped
6 to 8 curry leaves
1 teaspoon grated ginger
1 green chilli, finely chopped
1½ teaspoons oil
salt to taste

For the garnish
1 tablespoon chopped coriander leaves

1. Place the rawa in a microwave safe plate and microwave on HIGH for 1½ minutes.
2. Combine the oil, mustard seeds and urad dal in another microwave safe bowl and microwave on HIGH for 2 minutes.
3. Add the onions, curry leaves, ginger and green chilli, mix well and microwave on HIGH for 1½ minutes.
4. Heat 1½ cups of water in a microwave safe bowl for 1½ minutes and keep aside.
5. Add the rawa to the sautéed onions and mix well. Microwave on HIGH for 1½ minutes and add the salt and hot water and mix again.
6. Microwave on HIGH for 2 minutes, stirring once in between. Serve hot garnished with the chopped coriander.

RAWA IDLI

Picture on cover

Soft and spongy rawa idlis can be made in a jiffy for a quick and satiating breakfast.

Preparation time : 5 minutes.   Cooking time : 7 to 8 minutes.
Makes 12 idlis.

For the batter
1 cup rawa (semolina)
¼ cup curds
1 cup water
1 tablespoon chopped coriander
salt to taste

For the tempering
½ teaspoon mustard seeds (rai)
½ teaspoon cumin seeds (jeera)
a pinch asafoetida (hing)
1 teaspoon urad dal (split black lentils)
1 tablespoon broken cashewnuts
4 to 6 curry leaves
2 green chillies, chopped
1 teaspoon oil
½ teaspoon ghee

Other ingredients
¾ teaspoon unflavoured fruit salt
oil for greasing

For the batter
Combine all ingredients together, other than the fruit salt and leave aside for 10 minutes.

For the tempering
1. Combine the oil, ghee, mustard seeds, cumin seeds, urad dal and asafoetida in a microwave safe bowl and microwave on HIGH for 2 minutes.
2. Add the cashewnuts, curry leaves, green chillies and microwave for 1 more minute.

How to proceed
1. Pour 1 cup of water in the base of a microwave safe idli steamer and microwave on HIGH for 1 minute. Grease the idli moulds using little oil.
2. Add the tempering and the fruit salt to the batter and mix well.
3. Pour 2 tablespoons of batter into each greased cavity of the idli moulds and microwave, covered, on HIGH for 2 minutes.
4. Repeat with the remaining batter to make 8 more idlis.
   Serve hot with coconut chutney and sambhar.

Handy tips :
1. Fruit salt contains sodium so the salt has to added accordingly.
2. After adding fruit salt you have to make the idlis immediately as the fruit salt will loose its effect very soon and the idlis will not fluff up very well.
3. We have used plastic microwave safe idli stand with 8 idlis in each container. You can use small glass bowls instead and cover them with plastic (microwave safe) wrap to retain the moisture.
4. The time taken to cook the idlis will depend upon the number of idlis you make at a time.

GREEN PEAS DHOKLA

Picture on page 21

Easy and delicious dhoklas that are made nutritious with the addition of green peas. Serve them with green chutney to make a sumptuous breakfast.

**Preparation time : a few minutes.   Cooking time : 6 minutes.
Makes 1 dish.**

½ cup Bengal gram flour (besan)
½ cup green peas, boiled
1 teaspoon ginger-green chilli paste
1 tablespoon powdered sugar
½ cup water
¼ teaspoon citric acid (crystals)
¾ teaspoon unflavoured fruit salt
salt to taste

For the tempering
1 tablespoon oil
1 teaspoon mustard seeds (rai)
2 green chillies, finely chopped
a pinch asafoetida (hing)
1 tablespoon water

For the garnish
1 tablespoon chopped coriander
1 tablespoon grated coconut

1. Purée the green peas to a smooth paste using very little water.
2. Add all the other ingredients to the green pea paste and mix well. Add a little water, if required to get a dropping consistency.
3. Pour into a 150 mm. (6") diameter and 25 mm. (1") high greased microwave safe dish with a lid and microwave on HIGH for 3 minutes

covered.
4. Remove and let it stand for 2 minutes.

For the tempering
1. Combine the oil and the mustard seeds in a small microwave safe bowl and microwave on HIGH for 2 minutes.
2. Add the green chillies and asafoetida and microwave on HIGH for 1 more minute.
3. Remove from the microwave and add 1 tablespoon of water.

How to proceed
1. Pour the tempering over the dhoklas and cut into square pieces.
2. Garnish with the chopped coriander and grated coconut and serve hot with green chutney.

VARIATION : PALAK METHI DHOKLA
Replace the peas with ¼ cup of chopped palak and ¼ cup of chopped methi leaves and proceed as per the above recipe.

PANKI

Small rice pancakes steamed in-between banana leaves makes a great snack. The microwave version of the panki uses less oil compared to the conventional cooking method.

**Preparation time : 5 minutes.   Cooking time : 2 minutes.
Makes 12 pankis.**

⅓ cup rice flour (chawal ka atta)
1 tablespoon urad dal (split black lentils) flour
1 teaspoon curds
2 green chillies, finely chopped
½ teaspoon crushed cumin seeds (jeera)
1 teaspoon oil
salt to taste

Other ingredients
oil for greasing
2 to 3 banana leaves

For serving
green chutney

1. Cut the banana leaves into rectangles approx. 100 mm. x 75 mm. (4" x 3"), grease one side with oil and keep aside.
2. Combine all the ingredients for the panki in a bowl along with ¾ cup of water to make a thin batter.
3. Place one banana leaf rectangle on a microwave safe plate with the greased side facing up.
4. Spread 1½ tablespoons of the batter and place another leaf on top and press gently, taking care that the batter does not flow out of the leaf and is an even layer.

5. Repeat to make 11 more pankis and microwave on HIGH for 2 minutes. Serve hot with green chutney.

Handy tip : You may even arrange the pankis directly on the rotating tray.

ORANGE MARMALADE

Picture on page 31

Fresh orange juice and rind combine together to make this citrus preserve. Papaya added to jam helps to add bulk to a non-pulpy fruit like orange and also provides pectin which helps to thicken jams and preserves.

Preparation time : a few minutes.   Cooking time : 15 minutes.
Makes 1 cup.

---

1 cup fresh orange juice
1 cup papaya, grated
1 tablespoon orange rind
¼ cup sugar
a pinch citric acid mixed with 1 tablespoon orange juice

1. Combine all the ingredients except the citric acid mixture in a large microwave safe bowl and mix well.
2. Microwave on HIGH for 15 minutes stirring once in between.
3. Add the citric acid mixture and mix well.
4. Cool and store refrigerated in an air-tight container.

APPLE JAM

Picture on facing page

Rich amber coloured jam with a hint of lemon makes yummy accompaniment to fresh bread for breakfast.

**Preparation time : 5 minutes.   Cooking time : 4½ minutes.
Makes ½ cup.**

1½ cups apples, peeled and chopped
¼ cup sugar
1½ teaspoons lemon juice
a pinch cinnamon (dalchini) powder (optional)

1. Combine the apple and sugar in a microwave safe bowl and microwave on HIGH for 2 minutes.
2. Remove from the microwave and add the lemon juice and cinnamon powder. Mix well and microwave on HIGH for 2½ minutes.
3. Cool and store refrigerated in an air-tight container.

VARIATION : STRAWBERRY JAM

1. Substitute the apples for mashed strawberries to make fresh strawberry jam.
2. The quantity of sugar to be used will depend on how sweet the strawberries are.
3. The time taken to cook this jam will be slightly more than that for apple jam as the moisture content in strawberries is higher than that in apples.

1. ORANGE MARMALADE, Recipe on page 29
2. STRAWBERRY JAM, Recipe above
3. APPLE JAM, Recipe above

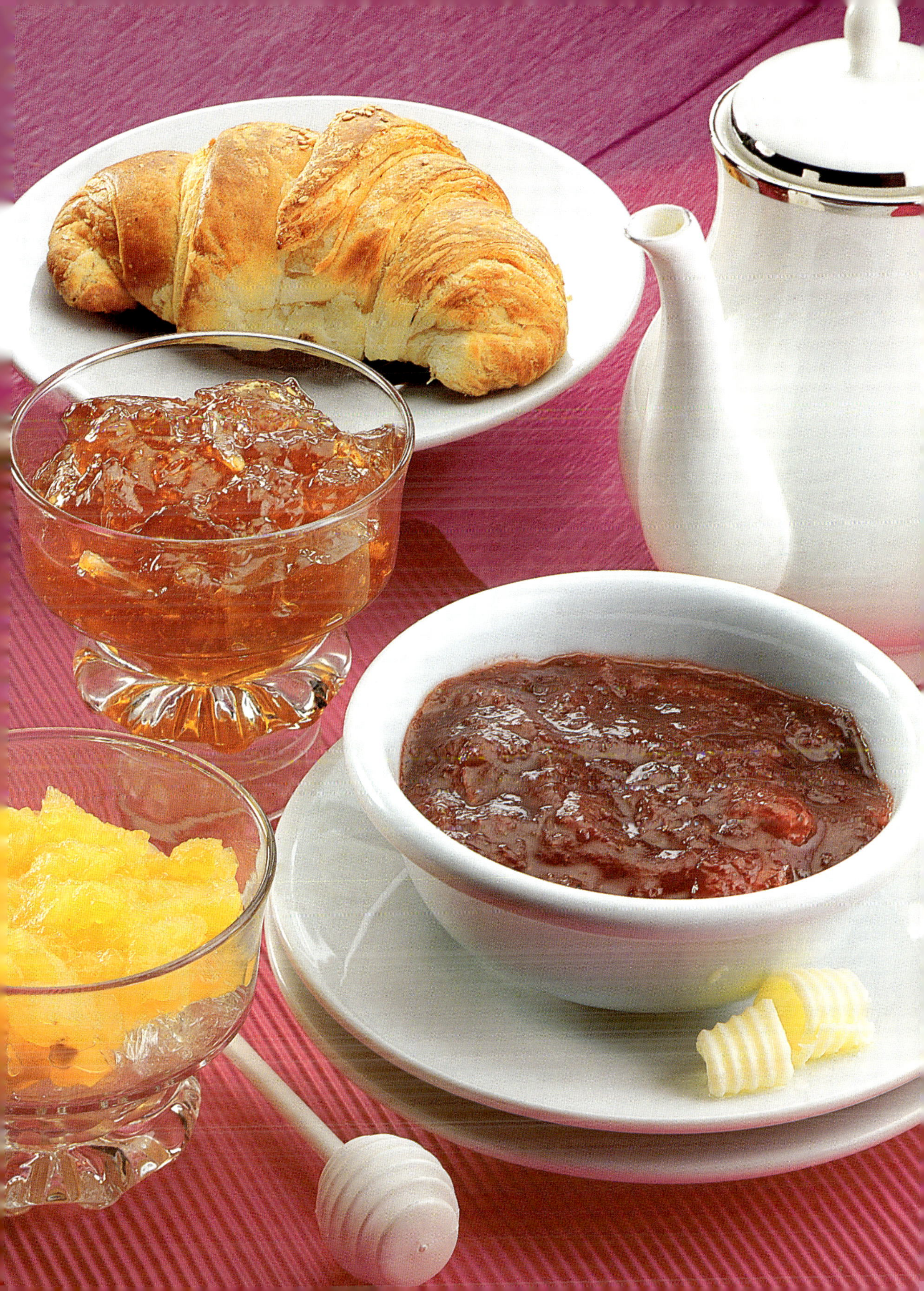

MAKAI SHEERA

Tender, sweet, fresh corn tempered with traditional Indian spices makes a quick and satiating breakfast.
You may also use frozen corn kernels when fresh corn is not available.

Preparation time : 10 minutes.   Cooking time : 6½ minutes.   Serves 2.
---

1 cup fresh corn, grated
½ teaspoon mustard seeds (rai)
½ teaspoon cumin seeds (jeera)
2 green chillies, slit
a pinch asafoetida (hing)
½ cup milk
½ teaspoon sugar
a few drops lemon juice
2 teaspoons oil
salt to taste

For the garnish
1 tablespoon chopped coriander

1. In a microwave safe bowl, mix the oil, mustard seeds and cumin seeds and microwave on HIGH for 2 minutes.
2. Add the green chillies and asafoetida and microwave on HIGH for 30 seconds.
3. Add the corn, mix well and microwave on HIGH for 2 minutes.
4. Add the milk, salt and sugar and microwave on HIGH for 2 minutes.
5. Add the lemon juice, mix well and serve garnished with the chopped coriander.

Handy tip : Approx. 3 medium size corn cobs will yield 1 cup grated corn.

JOWAR KHICHU

A traditional jowar flour snack flavoured with spices and garlic. Khichu is generally eaten alongwith pickle oil, but the sesame oil tastes just as good. If you wish to make this recipe ahead of time, remember to sprinkle a little water before reheating it in the microwave.

Preparation time : a few minutes.   Cooking time : 5 minutes.   Serves 2.

1 cup jowar flour (white millet flour)
1½ cups water
1 teaspoon ginger-green chilli paste
1 large clove garlic, grated
1 teaspoon sesame seeds (til)
1 teaspoon curds
1 teaspoon oil
salt to taste

To serve
1 tablespoon chopped coriander
1 teaspoon sesame (til) oil

1. Combine all the ingredients in a microwave safe bowl and mix well so that no lumps remain.
2. Microwave on HIGH for 5 minutes stirring every 1½ minutes. Serve hot garnished with the chopped coriander and sesame oil.

Tea-Time Treats

POHA CHIVDA

Picture on page 11

Crispy beaten rice flavoured with peanut and spices makes a delicious any time snack. This snack can be stored in an air-tight container for several days.

Preparation time : 10 minutes. Cooking time : 6 minutes.
Makes 3½ cups.

---

3 cups thin beaten rice (patla poha)
1 teaspoon mustard seeds (rai)
1 to 2 green chillies, finely chopped
4 to 6 curry leaves
1 tablespoon unsalted peanuts
2 tablespoons roasted chana dal (daria)
¼ teaspoon turmeric powder (haldi)
1 teaspoon powdered sugar
a pinch citric acid crystals
1 tablespoon oil
salt to taste

1. Place the poha in a shallow microwave safe dish and microwave on HIGH for 2 minutes. Keep aside.
2. In another microwave safe bowl, combine the oil and mustard seeds and microwave on HIGH for 2 minutes.
3. Add the green chillies, curry leaves, unsalted peanuts, roasted chana dal and turmeric powder and microwave on HIGH for 1 more minute.
4. Add this to the poha. Mix well and microwave on HIGH for 1 more minute.
5. Add the sugar, citric acid and salt and mix well.
6. Cool completely. Store in a air-tight container.

PAPAD POHA

Flaked rice and papad sautéed with spices and peanuts. Using thinner variety of poha known as patla poha or nylon poha, helps to make crispier snack.

> Preparation time : a few minutes.　　Cooking time : 4 minutes 20 sec.
> Makes 1½ cups.

5 small papads
1 cup thin beaten rice (patla poha)
½ teaspoon mustard seeds (rai)
1 tablespoon roasted chana dal (daria)
2 green chillies, slit
4 to 5 curry leaves
a pinch turmeric powder (haldi)
a pinch asafoetida (hing)
½ teaspoon powdered sugar
2 tablespoons oil
salt to taste

1. Place 5 papads separately on the microwave safe plate and microwave on HIGH for 20 seconds. Cool and crush.
2. Combine the papad and poha in microwave safe, flat plate and microwave on HIGH for 1 more minute.
3. In a 150 mm. (6") microwave safe bowl, combine the oil, mustard seeds and chana dal and microwave on HIGH for 2 minutes.
4. Add the green chillies, curry leaves, turmeric powder and asafoetida and microwave on HIGH for 1 more minute.
5. Add this to the papad poha mixture. Add salt and sugar and mix well.
6. Cool completely and store in an air-tight container.

BAKED PAPDI

An ideal low calorie alternative to the deep fried papdi. You can munch on these low calorie papdis anytime of the day. These baked papdis can be used to make sev puris and also as a base for canapés.

Preparation time : 5 minutes.   Cooking time : 2 minutes.
Makes 40 papadis.

¼ cup refined flour (maida)
½ teaspoon cumin seeds (jeera)
¼ teaspoon salt
1 teaspoon oil

1. Combine all the ingredients and knead into a firm dough using very little water.
2. Divide the dough into 40 equal parts.
3. Roll each portion into puris approx. 37 mm. (1½") in diameter.
4. Place 20 puris on a microwave safe dish taking care that the puris do not touch each other.
5. Prick the surface of each puri lightly with a fork and microwave on HIGH for 1 minute. Repeat the same for another 20 puris on another microwave safe dish.
6. Remove and let cool. Store in an air-tight container.

MASALA PEANUTS

Picture on page 11

Crunchy peanuts coated with a spicy besan mixture make a perfect accompaniment to a relaxed evening cup of tea.
Be very careful whilst cooking them as even a few extra seconds in the microwave will make the nuts hard and difficult to bite into.

Preparation time : 5 minutes.   Cooking time : 1½ minutes.
Makes 1 cup approx.

½ cup salted peanuts, unskinned
½ cup Bengal gram flour (besan)
2 teaspoons chilli powder
1 teaspoon fennel (saunf) powder
1½ teaspoons black salt (sanchal)
1 tablespoon oil
2 to 3 tablespoons water

1. Mix all the ingredients together in a bowl ensuring the batter coats the peanuts evenly.
2. On a greased microwave safe plate drop each of the coated peanuts separately and microwave on HIGH for 1½ minutes.
3. Remove and cool. Store in an air-tight container.

CINNAMON CRISPS

A yummy way to enjoy left over bread slices. Store the cinnamon crisps in an air-tight container and enjoy them with a hot cup of coffee.

> **Preparation time : a few minutes.   Cooking time : 4 minutes.**
> **Makes 16 pieces.**

4 slices bread

To be mixed together
1 tablespoon butter
1 tablespoon powdered sugar
½ teaspoon cinnamon (dalchini) powder

1. Apply the butter mixture on both sides.
2. Cut each slice into 4 strips vertically.
3. Place them on a microwave safe plate and microwave on HIGH for 4 minutes.
4. Cool completely and store in an air-tight container.

SOYA CRISPS

Picture on page 11

Replace your bag of potato chips with soya crisps for a healthy snack. The soya crisps serve as a good munchie when hunger strikes, a perfect snack for people on a diet.

> **Preparation time : a few minutes.   Cooking time : 10 minutes.
> Makes 1 cup.**

½ cup soyabeans
½ teaspoon turmeric powder (haldi)
1 teaspoon oil
1 teaspoon salt

1. Soak the soyabeans in water for 2 to 3 hours. Drain and discard the water.
2. Add the turmeric powder and salt to the soya beans, mix well and keep refrigerated overnight (6 to 8 hours).
3. Add 1 teaspoon oil to the beans, mix well and place ½ the beans in a shallow microwave safe plate and microwave on HIGH for 5 minutes, stirring once after 2½ minutes.
4. Repeat for the other half. Allow the soya crisps to come to room temperature and store in an air-tight container.

BESAN LADDOO

Making besan laddoos has never been so easy. Cook the gram flour and ghee mixture very carefully as even a few seconds extra can cause the gram flour to burn.

**Preparation time : 5 minutes.   Cooking time : 4 minutes.
Makes 10 laddoos.**

---

1 cup Bengal gram flour (besan)
⅓ cup ghee
¼ teaspoon cardamom (elaichi) powder
¾ cup powdered sugar

1. In a microwave safe bowl, add the gram flour and ghee and mix well. Microwave on HIGH for 3 minutes, stirring after every 1 minute.
2. Reduce the power to 70% and microwave for another minute stirring once after 30 seconds. Remove and let the mixture cool completely.
3. Add the cardamom powder and sugar and mix well.
4. Divide into 10 equal portions and shape into laddoos.

JEERA KAND WAFERS

Sweet potato waffers delicately flavoured with cumin seeds can be enjoyed even on days when you are fasting. Remember to place a muslin cloth or a thick tissue paper at the base of the plate before making the wafers as they tend to stick to the plate.

**Preparation time : 5 minutes.   Cooking time : 8 minutes.
Makes 1½ cups.**

2 cups peeled and thinly sliced kand (purple yam)
½ teaspoon roasted cumin seed (jeera) powder
salt to taste

1. Place a muslin cloth or a butter paper on a microwave safe plate and arrange half the kand slices separately on it.
2. Microwave on HIGH for 3 minutes turning them over once after 1½ minutes.
3. Sprinkle salt and cumin seed powder over the kand slices.
4. Microwave on HIGH for another minutes.
5. Repeat to make one more batch.
6. Cool completely and store in an air-tight container.

LOW CAL POTATO WAFERS

It's well worth the time and effort required to make these wafers for the amount of caloric intake it helps reduce. All the fun without the fat.

Preparation time : 5 minutes.   Cooking time : 10 minutes.
Makes 3 cups.
---

2 medium potatoes, peeled

To be mixed together
½ teaspoon oregano
1 teaspoon oil
salt to taste

1. Slice the potatoes using a wafer slicer.
2. Place a muslin cloth or a butter paper on a microwave safe plate and arrange half the potato slices separately on it.
3. Microwave on HIGH for 3 minutes turning them once after 1½ minutes.
4. Apply the salt and oregano mixture lightly on each of the potato slices.
5. Microwave on HIGH for another 2 minutes, turning them once after 1 minute.
6. Repeat to make one more batch.
7. Cool completely and store in an air-tight container.

BANANA PEPPER WAFERS

*Raw banana waffers flavoured with crushed pepper are simply delicious.
To get crisp waffers you have to slice the raw banana very thin. You may add a mixture of chaat masala and red chilli powder to make masala banana waffers.*

**Preparation time : a few minutes.　　Cooking time : 5 minutes.
Makes 1 cup.**

---

1 raw banana, peeled
salt to taste
½ teaspoon freshly ground pepper

1. Peel the banana and slice them using a wafer slicer.
2. Place them on a microwave safe plate lined with a butter paper.
3. Microwave them on HIGH for 3 minutes turning them over once after 1 minute.
4. Sprinkle salt and pepper and microwave on HIGH for 2 minutes.
5. Cool and store in an air-tight container.

SOYA NAMAK PARAS

Spiced crispies made of whole wheat and soya flour, ideal for those who have to cut down on fat. This is a lovely snack to be enjoyed while watching your favourite television programme.

Preparation time : 10 minutes. Cooking time : 4 minutes.
Makes 20 pieces.

¾ cup whole wheat flour (gehun ka atta)
¼ cup soya flour
¼ teaspoon turmeric powder (haldi)
½ teaspoon chilli powder
½ teaspoon coriander seed (dhania) powder
2 tablespoons oil
salt to taste

1. Combine all the ingredients in a bowl till it is a bread crumb like mixture.
2. Add approx. ¼ cup of water and knead lightly into a dough.
3. Roll out into a large chapatti approx. ¼ cm. thick.
4. Cut into diamond shapes or small puris using a cookie cutter.
5. Place on a lightly greased microwave safe plate and microwave on HIGH for 4 minutes.
6. Cool completely and store in air-tight container.

CHEESY CORNFLAKES

Kids will simply love the crispy cornflakes and crunchy peanuts flavoured with cheese and a hint of Worcestershire sauce. You may also use almonds instead of peanuts to make a healthier variation.

Preparation time : a few minutes.   Cooking time : 1½ minutes.
Makes 1½ cups.

---

1 cup cornflakes
¼ cup roasted peanuts
2 tablespoons grated cheese
¼ teaspoon chilli powder
½ teaspoon Worcestershire sauce
1 teaspoon butter
salt to taste

1. Combine the butter and peanuts in a microwave safe bowl and microwave on HIGH for 30 seconds.
2. Add all the other ingredients, mix well and microwave on HIGH for 1 more minute.
3. Cool completely and store in an air-tight container.

Children's Favourites

SINGAPORE NOODLES

Rice noodles and vegetables flavoured with curry powder and soya sauce make this oriental dish irresistible.

Rice noodles are very delicate and require practically no cooking. All you need to do is dunk them in hot water for a few minutes and then drain out the water and use them.

Preparation time : 10 minutes.　　Cooking time : 4½ minutes.　　Serves 4.

2 cups rice noodles
¼ cup onions, sliced
½ teaspoon chopped ginger
½ teaspoon chopped garlic
2 teaspoons chopped celery
¼ cup carrot, chopped
¼ cup capsicum, chopped
¼ cup bean sprouts
1½ teaspoons curry powder
1 teaspoon soya sauce
a pinch turmeric powder (haldi)
1 teaspoon sugar
salt and pepper to taste
1 teaspoon oil

For the garnish
¼ cup spring onion greens, chopped

1. PASTA WITH CHUNKY TOMATO SAUCE, Recipe on page 53
2. CHEESY NACHOS, Recipe on page 56

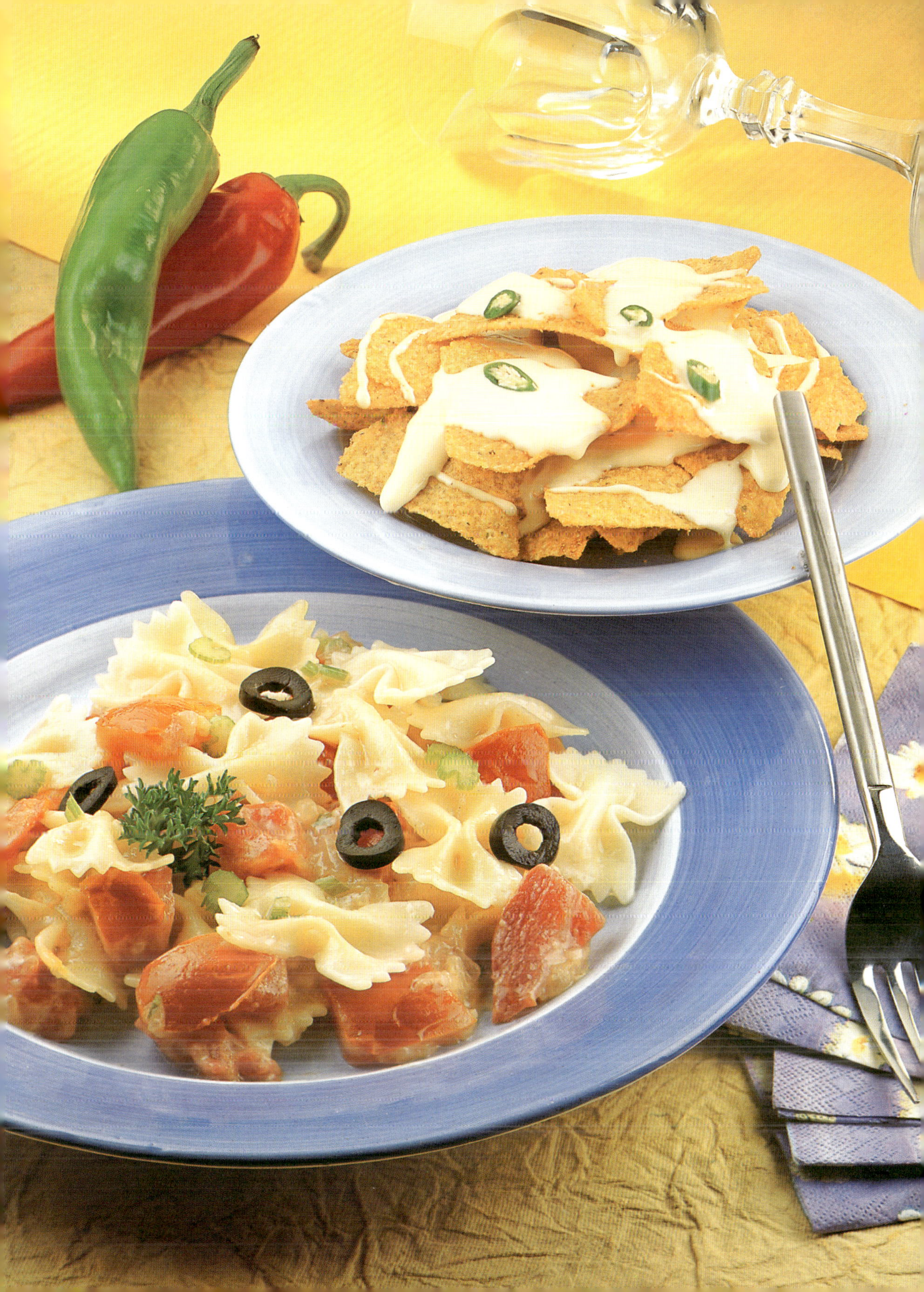

1. Microwave 2 cups of water in a microwave safe bowl, along with the turmeric powder on HIGH for 2 minutes.
2. Add the noodles and keep aside for 10 minutes till they are soft. Drain out all the excess water.
3. In another microwave safe bowl, combine the oil, onions, garlic, ginger and celery and microwave on HIGH for 30 seconds.
4. Add the carrots and capsicum and microwave on HIGH for 1 more minute.
5. Add the noodles, bean sprouts, curry powder, turmeric powder, soya sauce, sugar and salt and pepper and mix well. Microwave on HIGH for 1 more minute.

   Serve hot garnished with the chopped spring onion greens.

Handy tip : To make an easy substitute for curry powder, combine 1 teaspoon of dhania-jeera powder with a pinch of sambar powder and add it to this recipe.

MACARONI CHEESE

Macaroni, an elbow shaped pasta, has always been a favourite with kids. Macaroni mixed with vegetables and cheese and cooked with white sauce and herbs makes a tasty and wholesome meal that the kids are sure to love.

Preparation time : 5 minutes.   Cooking time : 11 minutes.   Serves 2.

1 cup macaroni
1½ cups water
1 teaspoon butter
1 large clove garlic, grated
¾ cup mixed vegetables (cauliflower, baby onions, French beans, carrots etc.), sliced
½ teaspoon cornflour
½ cup milk
2½ cheese slices
freshly ground pepper
¼ teaspoon mixed herbs
salt to taste

To serve
2 cheese slices

1. In a bowl, combine the macaroni, water, butter, garlic, vegetables and salt and microwave on HIGH for 8 minutes stirring once in between.
2. Combine the cornflour with 1 tablespoon milk and keep aside.
3. Add the cornflour mixture, milk and cheese and microwave on HIGH for 2 minutes.
4. Add the pepper and mixed herbs, mix well and microwave on HIGH for 1 more minute.

5. Top with the cheese slices, leave aside for 2 to 3 minutes and serve.

Note : The time taken to cook pasta will depend according to the brand and shape of pasta used.

PASTA WITH CHUNKY TOMATO SAUCE

Picture on page 49

Farfalle (bow-shaped pasta) tossed in a tomato basil sauce makes a quick and delicious snack to kids.
You may use any other pasta if the bow shaped one is not available. The time taken to cook will differ with the different shapes and sizes of the paste.

Preparation time : 10 minutes.   Cooking time : 19 minutes.   Serves 4.

¾ cup farfalle (bow-shaped pasta)
1 teaspoon oil
½ cup onions, finely chopped
3 large cloves garlic, finely chopped
1 tablespoon finely chopped celery
6 medium tomatoes
1 teaspoon basil or dried mixed herbs
1 tablespoon cream
1 teaspoon sugar
1 tablespoons olive oil
salt and pepper to taste

1. Make a criss cross slit on each tomato and place in a microwave safe plate and microwave on HIGH for 3 minutes.
2. Place them in a bowl of cold water and keep aside for 2 to 3 minutes.
3. Peel and quarter the tomatoes into 6 to 8 pieces. Remove and discard the seeds and keep the tomatoes aside.
4. In a medium sized microwave safe bowl, heat 1½ cups of water for 2 minutes.
5. Add 1 teaspoon oil and the pasta and microwave on HIGH for 5 minutes, stirring once in between.
6. Drain and pour cold water over the pasta to arrest cooking.

Drain and keep aside.
7. Combine the olive oil, onions, celery and garlic in a microwave on HIGH for 2 minutes.
8. Add the tomatoes and microwave on HIGH for 4 minutes.
9. Add the basil, salt, pepper and microwave on HIGH for 2 more minutes.
10. Add the cream and sugar and mix well.
11. Just before serving, add the pasta mix well and microwave on HIGH for 1 more minute.

Serve hot.

NOODLES WITH CREAMY MUSHROOMS

Noodles tossed in a mushroom and cheese sauce make this delightful recipe. Dried oregano lends a beautiful fragrance to the dish and complements the robust flavour of mushrooms.

| Preparation time : 10 minutes. | Cooking time : 9½ minutes. | Serves 2. |

½ cup noodles
¼ cup onions, chopped
¼ teaspoon finely chopped garlic
1 teaspoon plain flour (maida)
½ cup mushrooms, sliced
¼ teaspoon dried oregano
¾ cup milk
¼ cup water
1 tablespoon grated cheese
salt and pepper to taste
1 tablespoons butter

For the garnish
1 tablespoon chopped parsley

1. Heat butter in a microwave safe bowl for 20 seconds.
2. Add the onions and garlic and microwave on HIGH for 2 minutes.
3. Add the flour, mix well an microwave for ½ a minute.
4. Add the mushrooms, oregano, noodles, water and milk and mix well. Microwave for 6 minutes, stirring once every 2 minutes.
5. Add the salt and pepper, grated cheese and microwave for ½ a minute. Serve hot garnished with the chopped parsley.

CHEESY NACHOS

Picture on page 49

Ready-made nachos and cheese sauce make this snack irresistible, it is so wonderful that it is difficult to stop munching on this snack.

| Preparation time : a few minutes. | Cooking time : 3 minutes. | Serves 2. |

3 slices cheese
¼ cup milk
1 packet nachos
a pinch dried oregano (optional)

To serve
1 tablespoon chopped spring onion greens
dry red chilli flakes (paprika)

1. Mix the cheese and milk in a microwave safe bowl and microwave on HIGH for 3 minutes.
2. Mix well and add the oregano.
3. Pour over nachos and serve, sprinkled with the spring onion greens and dry red chilli flakes.

CHOCOLATE CARROT MUFFINS

A yummy tiffin box treat that's ready in one minute. Adding carrot to the chocolate muffins makes them more healthy for kids.

Preparation time : a few minutes.   Cooking time : 1 minute.
Makes 10 to 12 muffins.

½ cup melted butter
½ cup (½ can) condensed milk
2 teaspoons honey
2 tablespoons castor sugar
¾ cup carrot, grated
¾ cup plain flour (maida)
¼ teaspoon soda bi-carbonate
¼ teaspoon baking powder
2 tablespoons cocoa powder
2 tablespoons chopped walnuts
2 tablespoons raisins (kismis)
1 teaspoon vanilla essence
butter for greasing

Other ingredients
10 to 12 paper cups

For the garnish
1 tablespoon icing sugar

1. Mix all the ingredients in a bowl and pour 1 tablespoonful of the batter in each paper cup.
2. Arrange them on a microwave safe plate and microwave for 1 minute.

Allow it to stand for 5 minutes.
3. Just before serving, add the icing sugar in a strainer and dust over the muffins.

Handy tips : 1. The muffins may appear to be a little moist in the centre after cooking them for a minute. It is important to allow them to stand for at least 5 minutes as the heat retained within, will continue to cook the muffins.
2. The time taken to cook the muffins will vary with the size of the paper cups and the number of muffins to be cooked at a time.

ASPARAGUS BRUSCHETTA, Recipe on page 82

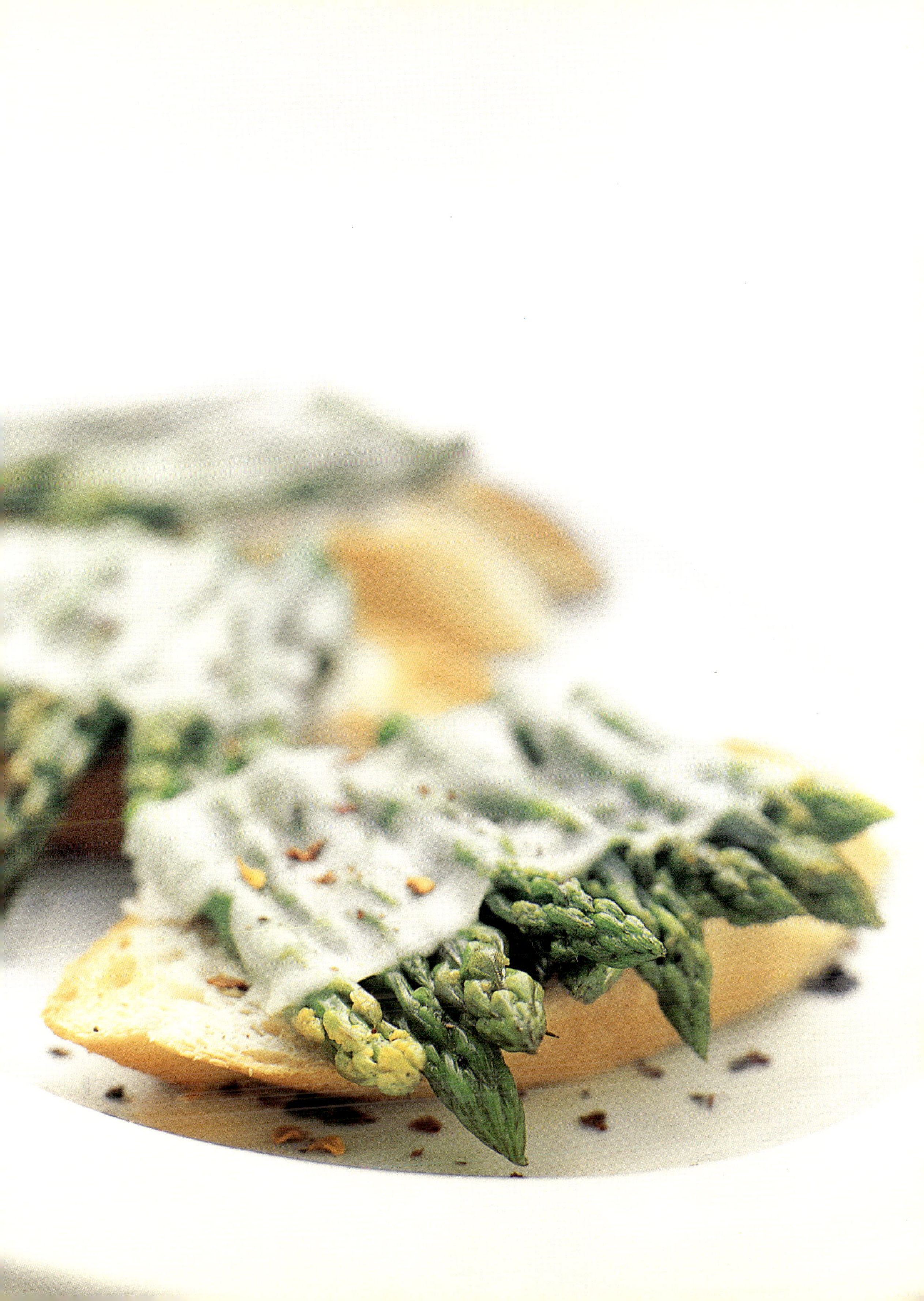

BAKED POTATOES

It takes about an hour in your regular oven but you can make baked potatoes in only 5 minutes in the microwave.
The scooped out potatoes, left-over form this recipe can be mashed and used to make a quick sandwich filling or tikkis.

Preparation time : 2 minutes. Cooking time : 5 minutes.
Makes 4 potatoes.

---

2 large potatoes
1 cup sweet corn kernels, boiled
1 tablespoon butter
2 tablespoons chopped onions
½ green chilli, finely chopped
2 tablespoons grated cheese
salt and pepper to taste

For the garnish
sprigs of parsley

1. Wash and prick the potatoes with the fork and microwave on HIGH for 5 minutes. Remove and cool.
2. Slit the potatoes into 2 halves. Scoop out the centre to make a small pocket and place them in a microwave safe bowl.
3. In another microwave safe bowl, heat the butter on HIGH for 30 seconds.
4. Add the onions, green chilli. Mix well and microwave on HIGH for 2 minutes.
5. Add the corn kernels, salt and pepper and mix well.
6. Spoon the mixture in the potatoes, sprinkle cheese and microwave on HIGH for 1 minute.
   Serve hot garnished with sprigs of parsley.

MOCK PIZZAS

Delicious pizzas ready in less than 2 minutes. Readymade burger buns make a quick substitute for the regular pizza base. The delightful flavours of onions, capsicum, tomatoes and cheese combine to make the topping for the mock pizzas.

Preparation time : 10 minutes.   Cooking time : 1 minute.
Makes 8 pizzas.

---

4 burger buns
2 tablespoons mozzarella cheese

To be mixed into a topping
1 cup tomatoes, finely chopped
2 tablespoons finely chopped onions
2 tablespoons finely chopped capsicum
½ teaspoon grated garlic
1 teaspoon finely chopped basil
1 green chilli, finely chopped
2 teaspoons ketchup
salt to taste

1. Cut the buns horizontally and microwave them on HIGH for 30 seconds.
2. Top with the filling mixture and sprinkle the cheese on top.
3. Microwave on HIGH for 30 seconds.
   Serve hot.

Snacks and Starters

FAT FREE DAHI WADA

Non-fried wadas dunked in yoghurt and topped with tangy imli chutney and cumin powder. This recipe is devised for people on a diet or for those who have to cut down on fat. Nevertheless, it is extremely good and very tasty.

> Preparation time : 1 hour.   Cooking time : 2½ minutes.
> Makes 8 dahi wadas.

For the wadas
½ cup yellow moong dal (split yellow gram)
1 to 2 green chillies
½ teaspoon unflavoured fruit salt
2 cups salted buttermilk
salt to taste
oil for greasing

For the curds
2 cups fresh thick curds
2 tablespoons milk
salt to taste

For the garnish
½ teaspoon chilli powder
1 teaspoon roasted cumin seed (jeera) powder
1 to 2 tablespoon khajur imli ki chutney
2 tablespoons chopped coriander

For the wadas
1. Soak the dal in warm water for at least 1 hour.
2. Drain out most of the water and grind it to a smooth paste in a blender along with the chillies and salt.
3. Add the fruit salt and mix well.

4. Pour 2 tablespoons of the batter into 8 small greased microwave safe bowls (2" diameter).
5. Microwave 4 at a time each batch for 1 minute and 15 seconds.
6. Remove and allow it to cool completely unmould.
7. Soak them in salted buttermilk for few minutes, till they are soft.
8. Drain and squeeze out any excess water.
9. Place on a serving plate.

How to proceed
1. Whisk the curds with the milk and salt and pour over the soaked wadas.
2. Garnish with the chilli powder, cumin powder, khajur imli ki chutney and chopped coriander.
   Serve chilled.

CREAMY MUSHROOM BUNS

A novel after school snack for your kids. A delicious and creamy mushroom mixture is filled in burger buns to make a quick snack. The mushroom filling can also be used to make pasta or as a topping on toasted bread for a yummy breakfast.

**Preparation time : 10 minutes.   Cooking time : 4 minutes.
Makes 4 buns.**

2 burger buns
¼ cup onions, chopped
1 small clove garlic, finely chopped
½ green chilli, finely chopped
1 cup mushrooms, sliced
¾ cup spinach (palak), finely chopped
¼ cup milk
¼ cup cheese, grated
¼ teaspoon dried oregano
1 tablespoon butter
salt and pepper to taste

For the topping
2 slices cheese

1. Cut each bun into 2 and scoop out the centre.
2. Soak the scooped bread in milk and keep aside.
3. In a microwave safe bowl combine the butter, onions, garlic and green chilli and microwave on HIGH for 30 seconds.
4. Add the mushrooms and microwave on HIGH for 2 minutes stirring once in between.
5. Add the spinach, milk, cheese, soaked bread, oregano, salt and pepper and microwave on HIGH for another minute.

6. Fill in the scooped bread cavity with the above mixture, top with cheese and microwave on HIGH for 30 seconds.
   Serve immediately.

Handy tip : You can use any other vegetables of your choice instead of the mushrooms.

CHILLI PANEER AND BABY CORN

A microwave variation of the ever so popular chilli paneer. Cottage cheese and baby corn tossed in an oriental soya based sauce makes a delicious starter. You may even serve this with fried rice as a main course or wrap it up in a thin chapati to make a yummy wrap.

Preparation time : 5 minutes.   Cooking time : 4½ minutes.   Serves 4.

---

1 cup paneer (cottage cheese), cut into 25 mm. (1") cubes
1 cup baby corn, cut into 25 mm. (1") pieces
⅓ cup spring onion whites, chopped
1 teaspoon chopped celery
3 to 4 green chillies, finely chopped
1 teaspoon chopped garlic
½ teaspoon chopped ginger
¼ cup capsicum, chopped
1 cup spring onion greens, finely chopped
1 tablespoon oil

To be mixed together into a soya sauce mixture
1½ teaspoons soya sauce
2 teaspoons cornflour
1 teaspoon sugar
salt and pepper to taste
¼ cup water

1. Put the baby corn in a microwave safe bowl. Sprinkle a little water and microwave on HIGH for 1 minute. Keep aside.
2. In another microwave safe bowl, combine the oil, spring onion whites, celery, green chillies, garlic, ginger and capsicum and microwave on HIGH for 2 minutes stirring once in between.

3. Add the paneer, baby corn and the soya sauce mixture. Mix well and microwave on HIGH for 1½ minutes stirring once in between.
4. Remove from the microwave, add the spring onion greens and mix well. Serve hot.

1. VEGETABLE SATAY WITH PEANUT SAUCE, Recipe on page 74
2. MIXED VEGETABLE STIR-FRY, Recipe on page 86

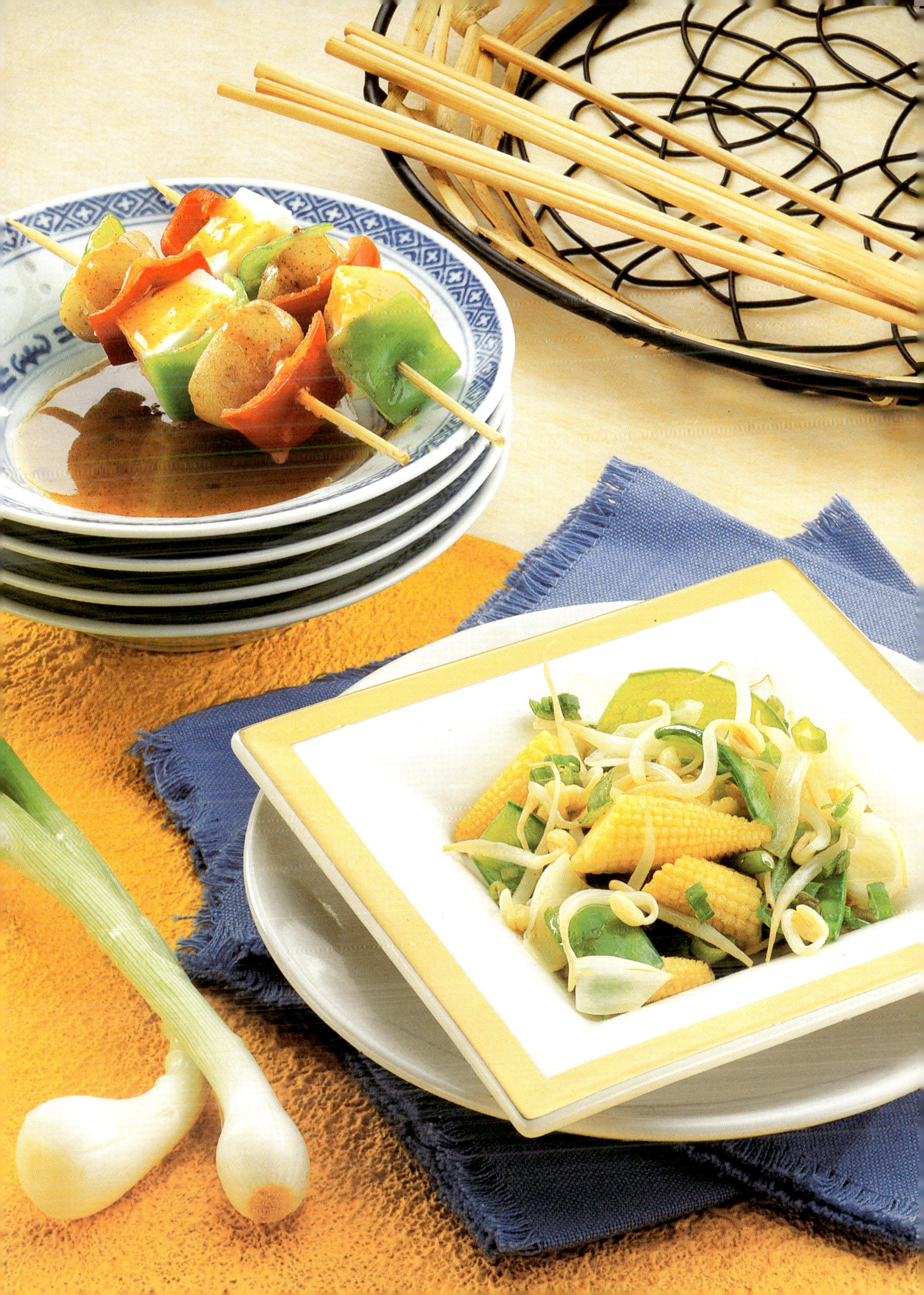

SPICY STUFFED POTATOES

Potato cups filled with a cheese vegetable mixture. I have used a mixture of mushrooms and peas for the stuffing, but you may use any combination of vegetables that strike your fancy. Remember to place a bowl of water in the centre of the microwave, while cooking the potatoes, to prevent them from dehydrating.

Preparation time : 10 minutes.   Cooking time : 8 minutes 45 seconds.
Makes 4 potatoes.

2 medium sized potatoes
¼ cup onions, chopped
⅓ cup mushroom / baby corn, finely chopped
1 to 2 green chillies, chopped
½ teaspoon grated ginger
1 tablespoon green peas, boiled
2 tablespoons chopped tomatoes
1 tablespoon butter
2 slices cheese
1 teaspoon butter for greasing the potatoes
salt and pepper to taste

For the garnish
1 tablespoon chopped coriander

1. Wash and prick the potatoes with a fork and microwave on HIGH for 5 minutes. Remove and cool.
2. Cut each potato into 2 halves and scoop out the centers.
3. Mash the scooped out potatoes and keep aside.
4. In a microwave safe bowl, combine the onions, mushrooms and butter and microwave on HIGH for 2 minutes stirring once in between.
5. Add the green chillies, ginger, green peas, scooped mashed potatoes, salt and pepper. Mix well and microwave on HIGH for 1 more minute.

6. Add the tomatoes, mix well and keep aside.
7. Rub some salt, pepper and butter on the skin.
8. Place them on a microwave safe plate and fill it with mushroom and pea mixture and microwave on HIGH for 15 seconds.
9. Remove and place ½ slice cheese on each half and microwave on HIGH for another 15 seconds.

   Serve immediately garnished with the chopped coriander.

MASALA PAV

This lip-smacking road-side chaat can be made in minutes in your microwave.

**Preparation time : 10 minutes.   Cooking time : 9 minutes 20 seconds.
Makes 4 pavs.**

4 ladi pavs
2 tablespoons butter

For the masala
1 cup onions, chopped
½ cup tomatoes, chopped
¼ cup capsicum, chopped
2 teaspoons finely chopped garlic
2 teaspoons finely chopped ginger
1 teaspoon finely chopped green chilli
a pinch turmeric powder (haldi)
1 teaspoon chilli powder
1 tsp black salt (optional)
2 tablespoons oil
salt to taste

For the garnish
2 tablespoons chopped coriander

To serve
onion rings
lemon wedges

For the masala
1. In a microwave safe bowl combine the oil, onions and garlic and microwave on HIGH for 4 minutes.

2. Add the tomatoes, ginger, green chilli, turmeric powder, chilli powder and black salt and microwave on HIGH for 3 minutes.
3. Add the capsicum and salt and microwave on HIGH for another 2 minutes.
4. Divide the masala mixture into 4 equal parts.

How to proceed
1. Cut each pav horizontally into 2.
2. Apply 1 teaspoon of butter on each slice of pav.
3. Spread the masala mixture on top and microwave on HIGH for 20 seconds.
4. Garnish with the chopped coriander and serve with onion rings and lemon wedges.

VEGETABLE SATAY WITH PEANUT SAUCE

Picture on page 69

A medley of vegetables and paneer threaded on wooden skewers and flavoured with a sweet and spicy peanut sauce makes a lip smacking snack.

Preparation time : 10 minutes.   Cooking time : 5 minutes 30 seconds.
Makes 4 satays.

For the vegetable satay
4 satay sticks or wooden skewers
8 cubes of paneer (25 mm. (1") dices)
8 pieces baby corn (25 mm. (1") dices)
8 pieces onions (25 mm. (1") cube)
8 cubes capsicum (25 mm. (1") dices)

For the satay marinade
1 teaspoon curry powder
1 tablespoon oil
1 teaspoon lemon juice
salt to taste

For the peanut sauce
1 tablespoon chopped onions
1 clove garlic, chopped
½ cup roasted peanut powder
½ teaspoon chilli powder
¼ cup water
½ teaspoon soya sauce
½ teaspoon jaggery (gur)
1½ teaspoons lemon juice
salt to taste
1 teaspoon butter

For the satay sticks

1. In a microwave safe bowl mix add the capsicum and baby corn along with 1 teaspoon water and microwave on HIGH for 1½ minutes. Remove and keep aside.
2. Combine all the ingredients for the satay marinade in a bowl and add the paneer, baby corn, onions and capsicum and marinate for 10 minutes.
3. Thread the paneer, baby corn, onions and capsicum alternatively on 4 satay sticks or wooden skewers.

For the peanut sauce

1. Combine the onions, garlic and butter in a microwave safe bowl and microwave on HIGH for 30 seconds.
2. Add the peanut powder and chilli powder and microwave on HIGH for 30 seconds.
3. Add the water, soya sauce, jaggery, lemon juice and salt, mix well and microwave on HIGH for 1½ minutes. Keep aside.

How to proceed

1. Place the satay on a greased microwave safe flat plate, pour the satay sauce over and microwave on HIGH for 1 minute.
2. Remove and spoon the sauce back from the plate and microwave on HIGH for another 30 seconds.
Serve hot.

Handy tip : If the satay sauce becomes a little thick add some water to thin down its consistency.

MEDITERRANEAN CROSTINI

This delicious olive, cheese and tomato topped bread is perfect for parties, buffets and makes a welcome appetizer.
It also makes a perfect accompaniment to pasta, soup or any other continental main course.

Preparation time : 5 minutes.   Cooking time : 30 seconds.
Makes 6 crostinis.

---

6 slices French bread
¼ cup black olives, sliced
¼ cup cheese, grated
1 tablespoon butter

To be mixed together for the marinated tomatoes
12 thin slices of tomatoes
1 teaspoon chopped basil
½ teaspoon chopped garlic
1 teaspoon olive oil
salt to taste
freshly crushed pepper to taste

1. Butter the bread slices. Top each slice with 2 slices of the marinated tomatoes.
2. Sprinkle with the olives and cheese and microwave on HIGH for 30 seconds.
   Serve hot.

VARIATION : FOR THE GRILL OPTION
At step 1, pre-heat the oven to 250°C (500°F) and bake the bread slices for 3 minutes before adding the topping.

QUICK CHEESY FONDUE

Picture on page 79

Cheese spread and milk combine to give a creamy fondue almost instantly.
Fondue pots are available in cast iron and ceramic at specialty stores. I personally prefer to use the cast iron ones as the fondue does not stick down as in the ceramic pots.
Sautéed vegetables like broccoli, potatoes, mushrooms and pickled olives make good accompaniments for the fondue.

> **Preparation time : a few minutes.   Cooking time : 4 minutes.**
> **Makes 2 cups.**

1 cup milk
¾ cup cheese spread
2 tablespoons cornflour
1 teaspoon chopped onions
½ teaspoon freshly ground pepper
salt to taste
1 teaspoon butter

1. Dissolve the cornflour in 2 tablespoons of cold milk. Keep aside.
2. Combine the butter and onions in a microwave safe bowl and microwave on HIGH for 1 minute.
3. Add the milk, cheese spread, cornflour mixture and salt. Mix well and microwave on HIGH for 3 minutes stirring once in between.
4. Sprinkle the pepper and mix well.
   Serve hot with crisp bread and buttered vegetables.

PAHADI PANEER TIKKA

Paneer, capsicum, onions and potatoes dunked in a rich curd based, mint flavoured marinade makes a delicious starter.
To make a thick marinade you need to start with thick curds. In case the marinade is too runny, add a spoonful of besan to the mixture.

Preparation time : 10 minutes.   Cooking time : 5 minutes.   Serves 4.

For the tikka
½ cup capsicum, diced
½ cup onions, diced
½ cup paneer, diced
3 to 4 baby potatoes, boiled and unpeeled

For the marinate
¼ cup mint, chopped
½ cup coriander, chopped
5 to 6 cashewnuts
¼ cup thick curds
2 to 3 green chillies
25 mm. (1") ginger
1 teaspoon mustard oil
salt to taste

To serve
tomato slices
lemon wedges

QUICK CHEESE FONDUE, Recipe on page 77

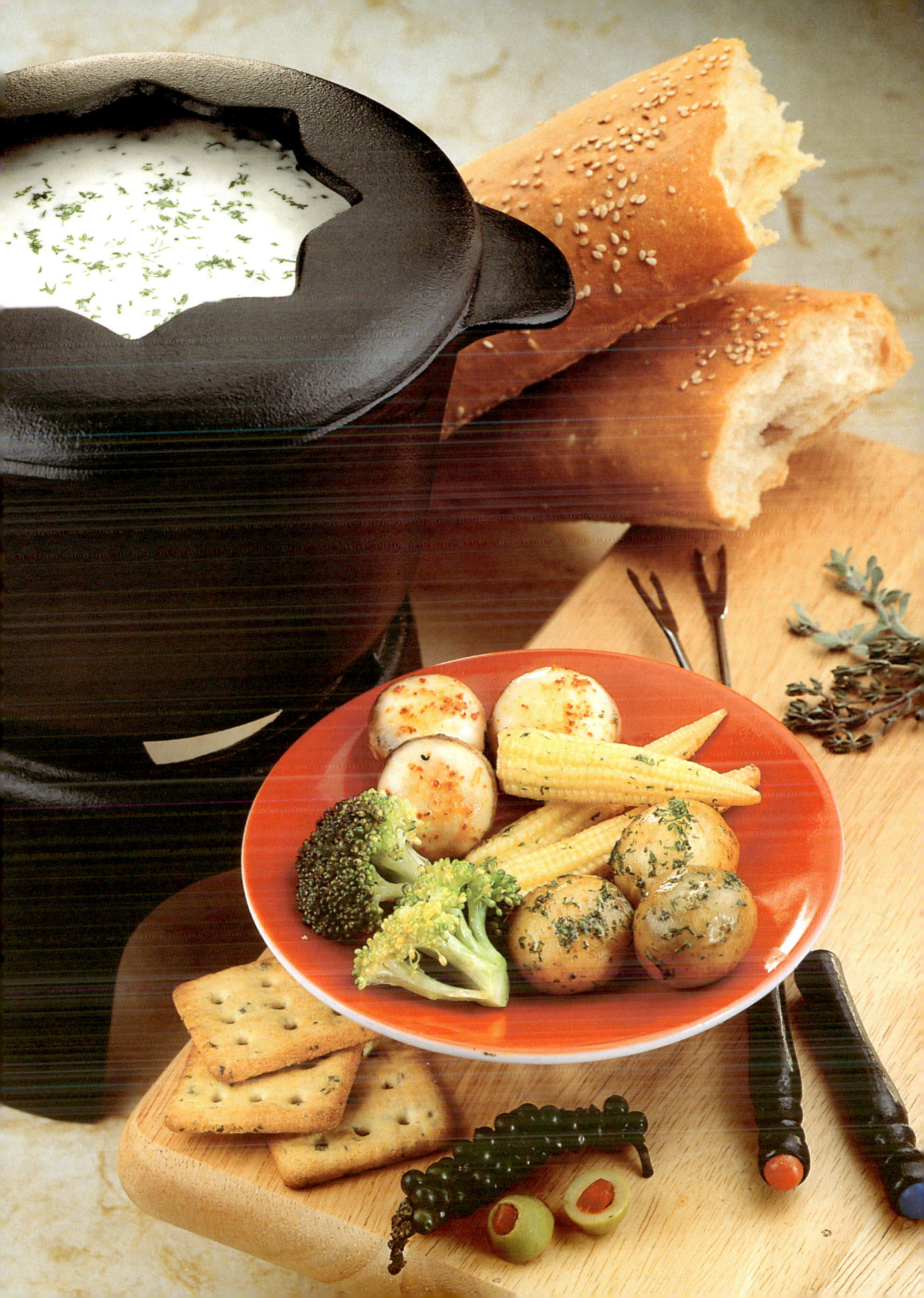

For the marinate
1. Grind together the mint, coriander, cashewnuts, green chillies and ginger.
2. Mix the coriander paste with the curds, mustard oil and salt. Keep aside.

For the tikka
1. Add the capsicum, onions, paneer and potatoes to the marinade and leave aside for ½ an hour.
2. Thread a piece of onion, potato, capsicum and paneer each onto a wooden skewer. Repeat till all the pieces are used up.

How to proceed
1. Place the skewers into a microwave safe shallow plate and microwave on HIGH for 3 minutes.
2. Remove and spoon the marinate from the plate back onto the tikkas and microwave on HIGH for another 2 minutes.
Serve hot with tomato slices and lemon wedges.

VARIATION : FOR THE GRILL OPTION
1. Pre-heat the microwave, using the microwave and grill option, to 250°C (500°F) for approximately 9 minutes.
2. Place the tikkas onto a microwave safe shallow plate and microwave on HIGH for 5 minutes.
Serve hot.

DAINTY SPINACH DUMPLINGS

A light, vitamin-rich snack for spinach lovers made using the calorie reducing steaming technique.

Preparation time : 10 minutes.   Cooking time : 2 minutes.
Makes 6 pieces.

---

2 cups spinach (palak), finely chopped
1 green chilli, finely chopped
2 tablespoons gram flour (besan)
2 teaspoons whole wheat flour (gehun ka atta)
2 teaspoons fresh curds (optional)
a pinch asafoetida (hing)
1 teaspoon sugar
¼ teaspoon soda bi-carb
1 teaspoon oil
salt to taste

To serve
green chutney

1. Mix all the ingredients, using curds if the mixture is too dry for shaping.
2. Divide the mixture into 18 equal portions and place on a large greased microwave safe plate. Cover with a damp muslin cloth and microwave on HIGH for 2 minutes.
3. Keep aside for 2 to 3 minutes.
4. Lift gently using a flat knife and place onto a serving plate. Serve with green chutney.

ASPARAGUS BRUSCHETTA

Picture on page 59

Crispy French bread slices topped with asparagus and cheese. The bruschettas can be served as a snack or as an accompaniment to soup. Choose slender, bright green asparagus to make these bruschetta.

**Preparation time : 10 minutes.   Cooking time : 1 minutes 45 seconds.
Makes 4 bruschettas.**

---

4 French bread slices
24 spears asparagus, cut 50 mm. (2") long
2 tablespoons grated mozzarella cheese
1 teaspoon chopped parsley
1 teaspoon butter
a pinch dry red chili flakes (paprika)
salt to taste

1. In a microwave safe bowl, add the asparagus spears alongwith 1 tablespoon of water and salt and microwave on HIGH for 45 seconds. Remove and keep aside.
2. Mix together the butter and parsley and apply the mixture on one side of each of the 4 slices.
3. Place the buttered slices on a shallow microwave safe plate and microwave on HIGH for 30 seconds.
4. Arrange 6 asparagus spears on each slice, top with the grated cheese and dry red chilli flakes and microwave on HIGH for 30 seconds.
Serve immediately.

HERB POTATOES

Succulent baby potatoes coated with dill, parsley and cheese. The herb potatoes can be enjoyed as cocktail snack or as an accompaniment to a main course or with cheese fondue. Quick as a wink to prepare, everyone is sure to enjoy these delicious, cheesy herb flavoured potatoes.

Preparation time : 10 minutes.   Cooking time : 6½ minutes.   Serves 4.

---

1 cup (approx. 8 to 10) baby potatoes
2 teaspoons dill (suva bhaji)
2 teaspoons chopped parsley
1 tablespoon grated mozzarella cheese
2 teaspoons butter
salt and pepper to taste

1. Wash the baby potatoes and pierce them gently with a fork.
2. Place the potatoes in a microwave safe bowl and microwave on HIGH for 5 minutes. Remove and allow the potatoes to stand for 2 to 3 minutes.
3. Cut each potato into 2 and keep aside.
4. In another microwave safe bowl, mix together the butter, dill and parsley and microwave on HIGH for 30 seconds.
5. Add the potatoes, salt and pepper and mix well.
6. Sprinkle the grated cheese and microwave on HIGH for 45 seconds. Serve hot.

Handy tip : While cooking potatoes, in the microwave it is advisable to place a small bowl of water along with the potatoes in the microwave, in order to prevent the potatoes from drying out.

SPICED BABY CORN AND BROCCOLI

Baby corn and broccoli cooked in a fragrant spice mix makes a delectable starter. You may even serve this as a vegetable with steamed rice to make a satiating meal.

Preparation time : 5 minutes.   Cooking time : 5 minutes.   Serves 2.

1 cup baby corn, cut into 25 mm. (1") pieces
1 cup broccoli florets
2 tablespoons chopped onions
½ teaspoon chopped garlic
¼ cup tomatoes, chopped
1 teaspoon plain flour (maida)
½ cup milk
1 teaspoon butter
salt to taste

To be ground together into a spice powder
1 teaspoon dry mixed herbs
3 peppercorns
¼ teaspoon dry red chilli flakes (paprika) powder

1. In a microwave safe bowl, combine together baby corn and broccoli alongwith 2 tablespoons of water and microwave on HIGH for 1 minute. Remove and keep aside.
2. In another microwave safe bowl add the butter, onions and garlic and microwave on HIGH for 1 minute.
3. Add the tomatoes, plain flour and the spice powder, mix well and microwave on HIGH for 1 minute.

4. Add the milk, baby corn, broccoli and salt, mix well and microwave on HIGH for 2 minutes.
   Serve hot.

Tip : You can make your own dry mixed herb mix by adding together equal proportions of dry herbs like oregano, rosemary and thyme.

MIXED VEGETABLE STIR-FRY

Picture on page 69

Fresh vegetables like baby corn, snow peas and bean sprouts are tossed together in garlic to make this delectable stir-fry. The cornflour and water mixture helps to make a thick sauce which coats the veggies lightly and prevents them from drying out.

Preparation time : 10 minutes.   Cooking time : 4 minutes.   Serves 2.

½ cup baby corn, cut into 25 mm. (1") pieces
½ cup snow peas, cut into 25 mm. (1") pieces
½ cup bean sprouts
¼ cup spring onion greens, chopped
¼ cup spring onion whites, chopped
½ teaspoon chopped garlic
½ teaspoon chopped green chillies
½ cup water
1 teaspoon corn flour mixed with 1 teaspoon water
1 teaspoon oil
a pinch sugar
salt and pepper to taste

1. In a microwave safe bowl, combine together baby corn, snow peas and bean sprouts along with 2 tablespoons of water and microwave on HIGH for 1 minute. Remove and keep aside.
2. In another microwave safe bowl, add the oil, spring onion whites, garlic and green chillies and microwave on HIGH for 1 minute.
3. Add the water, cornflour mixture, cooked vegetables, spring onion greens, sugar, salt and pepper, mix well and microwave on HIGH for 2 minutes. Serve hot.

ALOO KAND CHAAT

Potato and yam cubes tossed in a chatpata masala make a tongue-tickling starter. Adding a teaspoon of water while cooking the potatoes and yam helps to prevent the vegetables from dehydrating in the microwave.

Preparation time : 10 minutes.   Cooking time : 6 minutes.   Serves 4.

---

1 cup potato, peeled and cubed
1 cup kand (purple yam), peeled and cubed
¼ cup onions, finely chopped
¼ cup coriander, chopped
2 tablespoons chopped mint
1 teaspoon butter

To be mixed together into a masala
½ teaspoon chilli powder
1 teaspoon roasted cumin seed (jeera) powder
½ teaspoon dry mango powder (amchur)
½ teaspoon black salt (sanchal)
½ teaspoon sugar

1. Combine the potatoes, kand and butter in a bowl, add 1 teaspoon of water and mix well and microwave on HIGH for 6 minutes, stirring once in between after 3 minutes.
2. Add the onions, coriander, mint and the mixed masala and mix well. Serve immediately.

PANEER BHURJI

Tastes great when fresh home-made paneer is used. You can serve the paneer bhurji on toasted bread or baked papdi to make a quick snack.

Preparation time : 10 minutes.   Cooking time : 10 minutes.
Makes 4 papdis.

---

1 cup paneer (cottage cheese), grated
½ cup onions, chopped
¼ cup capsicum, chopped
½ teaspoon finely chopped ginger
½ teaspoon finely chopped garlic
1 to 2 green chillies, finely chopped
a pinch turmeric powder (haldi)
a pinch black salt (sanchal)
2 tablespoons chopped coriander
2 tablespoons chopped mint
1 teaspoon lemon juice
1 teaspoon oil
salt to taste

To serve
15 to 20 baked papdis, page 37

GARAM GOLPAPDI, Recipe on page 111

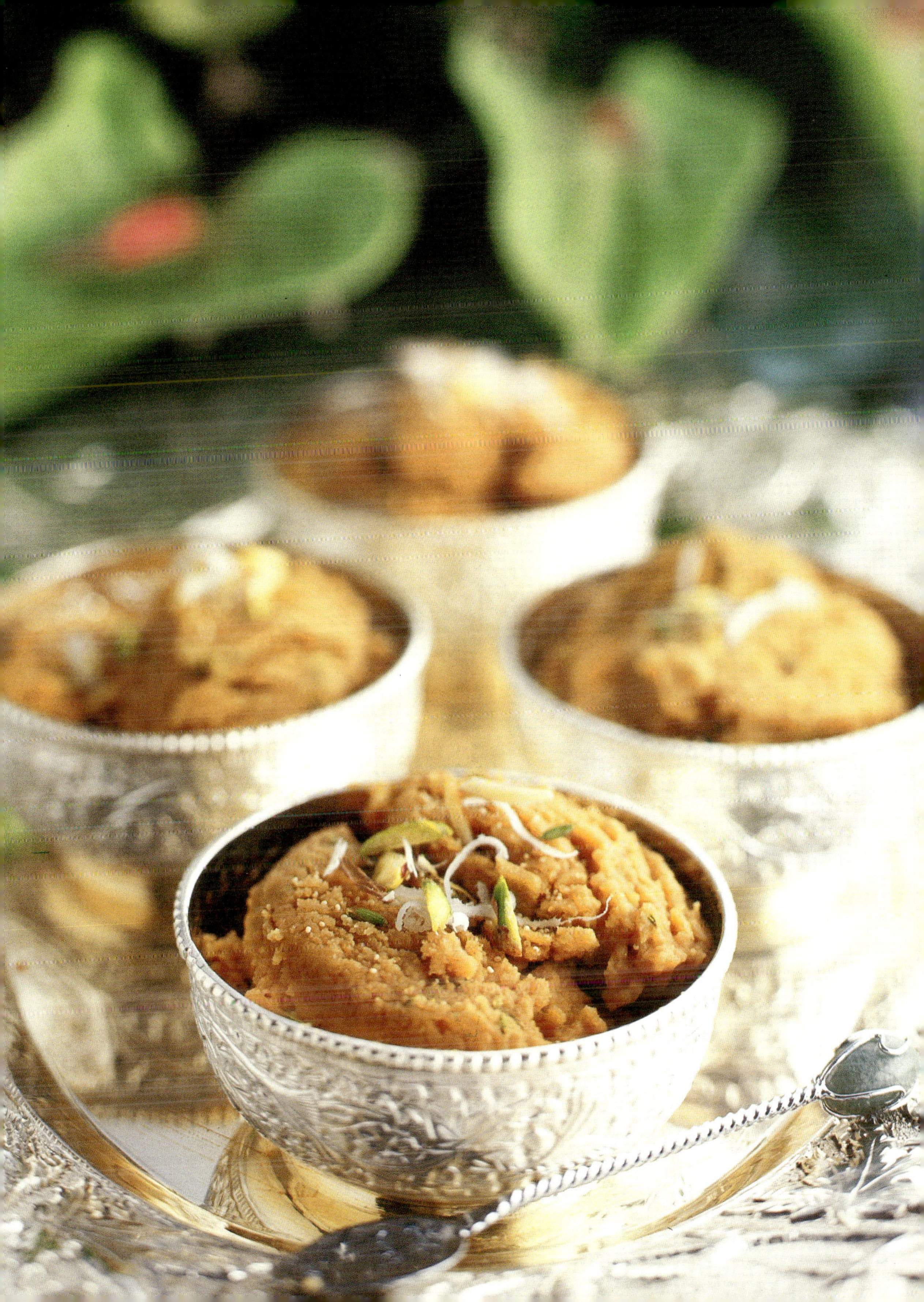

For the garnish
2 tablespoons chopped coriander

1. In an microwave safe bowl combine the oil, onions, ginger, garlic together and mix well. Microwave on HIGH for 4 minutes.
2. Add the capsicum, green chillies, turmeric powder and black salt and microwave on HIGH for 2 minutes.
3. Add the paneer, coriander, mint, lemon juice and salt and mix well.
4. Serve the bhurji topped on baked papdis or toasted bread slices, garnished with chopped coriander.

Dips and Drinks

CHUNKY BROCCOLI AND CORN DIP

A delicious dip with a bounty of vegetables. Serve it as an appetizer with crackers or breadsticks or you can also toss in some cooked pasta to make a filling main course.

**Preparation time : 10 minutes.   Cooking time : 4½ minutes.
Makes 1cups.**

¼ cup broccoli florets
¼ cup corn kernels
½ cup milk
2 teaspoons chopped onions
a pinch dry red chilli flakes (paprika)
1 teaspoon plain flour (maida)
2 teaspoons butter
salt to taste

1. In a microwave safe bowl, add the broccoli florets and corn kernels along with 1 tablespoon of water and microwave on HIGH for 45 seconds.
2. In another microwave safe bowl, add the butter, onions and dry red chilli flakes and microwave on HIGH for 1 minute.
3. Add the flour, mix well and microwave on HIGH for 30 seconds.
4. Add the milk, broccoli, corn kernels and salt and microwave on HIGH for 2 minutes.
   Serve warm.

BABA GHANOUJ

There's definitely more to lebanese cuisine than 'Hummus'. Brinjals, sesame, curds and garlic combine together to make this delectable Middle-Eastern dip. After tasting this dip people will definitely strike brinjals off their do-not-like vegetable list.

**Preparation time : 10 minutes.   Cooking time : 2 minutes.
Makes 1 cup.**

1/3 cup white sesame (til) paste
1/3 cup brinjal, peeled and chopped
1/3 cup curds
1/4 teaspoon chopped garlic
1 tablespoon olive oil
1 tablespoon chopped mint
1/4 teaspoon lemon juice
salt to taste

For the garnish
1 tablespoon sliced olives
3 to 4 sprigs of mint

1. In a greased microwave safe dish place the brinjal and microwave on HIGH for 2 minutes. Cool, mash to a pulp and keep aside.
2. Combine all the other ingredients together in another bowl and mix well.
3. Lightly fold in the brinjal pulp. Refrigerate till chilled.
4. Garnish with olives and mint springs and serve with pita bread or cream cracker biscuits.

Handy tip : Grind the sesame seeds with a little water in a blender to make a smooth paste.

BENGALI TOMATO CHUTNEY

A tangy tomato chutney flavoured with panch phoran seeds. Panch Phoran is a Bengali blend of spices containing equal parts of mustard seeds, kalonji, cumin seeds, saunf and fenugreek seeds.

Preparation time : 10 minutes.   Cooking time : 15 minutes.
Makes 1 cup.

---

2 cups tomatoes, cut in large cubes
¼ teaspoon panch phoran seeds
1 tablespoon raisins (kismis), soaked
½ teaspoon ginger, cut into thin strips
1 teaspoon chopped green chillies
1 tablespoon sugar
1 teaspoon oil or mustard oil
salt to taste

1. Heat the oil in a microwave safe bowl for 1 minute.
2. Add the panch phoran seeds and microwave for 1 minute.
3. Add the tomatoes and salt and mix well. Cover and microwave on HIGH for 3 more minutes.
4. Add the raisins, ginger, green chillies and sugar and microwave for 10 minutes stirring twice in between after every 4 minutes.
5. Cool and store refrigerated in an air-tight container.

BARBEQUE DIP

No barbeque party can be complete without this tangy, tongue-tickling dip. A very easy to make, no-fuss dip.

**Preparation time : 5 minutes. Cooking time : 6 minutes.
Makes 1½ cups.**

½ cup ketchup
½ cup onions, finely chopped
2 tablespoons Worcestershire sauce
1 tablespoon vinegar
1 tablespoon lemon juice
¼ cup butter
¼ teaspoon dry red chilli flakes (paprika)
½ cup water
2 tablespoons sugar
1 teaspoon cornflour mixed with 1 tablespoon water
½ teaspoon pepper
1 teaspoon salt

1. Combine all the ingredients except the cornflour paste in a deep microwave safe bowl and mix well.
2. Microwave on HIGH for 4 minutes stirring once in between after 2 minutes.
3. Add the cornflour paste, mix well and microwave on HIGH for 2 more minutes.
   Serve at room temperature with grilled vegetables.

CREAMY CHEESE DIP

A cheese dip delicately flavoured with capsicum and mustard. This creamy dip compliments beautifully with most deep fried starters like wafers, nachos, croquettes etc.

**Preparation time : 2 minutes.   Cooking time : 2 minutes.
Makes ¾ cups.**

½ cup milk
4 cheese slices
2 tablespoons finely chopped capsicum
½ teaspoon cornflour
¼ teaspoon prepared mustard paste
salt to taste

1. In a microwave safe bowl, add the milk, cheese slices, capsicum and cornflour, mix well and microwave on HIGH for 2 minutes, stirring once after 1 minute. Remove and allow it cool.
2. Add the mustard paste and salt and mix well.

KOKUM SHERBET

This soothing refresher is an excellent cure for acidity.

Preparation time : 5 minutes.   Cooking time : 7 minutes.
Makes 6 to 8 glasses.

1½ cup semi-dried kokum
1 cup sugar
1 teaspoon cumin seed (jeera) powder
½ teaspoon black salt (sanchal)
a pinch of citric acid

1. Combine the kokum with 1 cup of water in a microwave safe bowl and microwave on HIGH for 1 minute. Keep aside for about 10 minutes. Drain and preserve the kokum water.
2. Purée the kokum in a blender using ½ cup of the preserved kokum water, to obtain a smooth purée.
3. Combine the sugar with the remaining kokum water and microwave on HIGH for 6 minutes stirring once in between after 3 minutes to get a syrup of 1 stiring consistency.
4. Add the puréed kokum and strain through a sieve.
5. Add the cumin seed powder, black salt and citric acid and mix well.
6. Cook completely and store refrigerated in an air tight container.

How to proceed

When you wish to serve, take 3 to 4 tablespoons of this mixture in a glass and top it with water and ice.

PANHA

Picture on page 11

A delicious summer cooler made from raw mangoes, flavoured with cardamom and saffron.

> **Preparation time : 5 minutes. Cooking time : 4 minutes.**
> **Makes 4 to 6 glasses.**

1 cup raw mangoes, peeled and cubed
½ cup sugar
½ teaspoon cardamom (elaichi) powder
a few strands saffron mixed with 1 tablespoon water

1. Combine the mangoes with ½ cup water in a microwave safe bowl and microwave on HIGH for 2 minutes.
2. Add the sugar and microwave on HIGH for another 2 minutes.
3. Add the cardamom powder and mix well. Cool completely.
4. Grind in a blender to make a smooth purée. Add the saffron mixture and mix well.
5. Store refrigerated in an air-tight container.

How to proceed
When you wish to serve, take 3 to 4 tablespoons of this mixture in a glass and top it with water and ice and serve immediately.

SAUNF SHERBET

A delicious cooling drink for summers which helps keep dehydration at bay.

Preparation time : 5 minutes.   Cooking time : 8 minutes.
Makes 3 to 5 glasses.

½ cup fennel seeds (saunf)
½ cup sugar

1. Blend the fennel seeds and sugar to a fine powder.
2. Combine this powder with 1 cup water in a microwave safe bowl and microwave on HIGH for 8 minutes stirring twice in between.
3. Keep aside for about 10 minutes.
4. Cool completely and stain through a sieve.
5. Store refrigerated in an air-tight container.

How to proceed

When you wish to serve, take 3 to 4 tablespoons of this mixture in a glass and top it with water and ice.
Serve Immediately.

Indian Desserts

PINEAPPLE KESARI

Picture on page 107

A subtly flavoured sheera that has the goodness of pineapples which makes an interesting variation to the sweet sheera. Choose ripe pineapple for best results.
It is necessary to cook the pineapples, before adding to the sheera, in order to reduce the acidic content of the fruit.

Preparation time : 10 minutes.   Cooking time : 10 minutes.   Serves 2.

½ cup semolina (rawa)
½ cup pineapple purée
½ cup milk
1 cup water
5 tablespoons sugar
a few strands saffron with 1 tablespoon milk
2 teaspoons ghee
¼ teaspoon cardamom (elaichi) powder

1. In a microwave safe bowl mix together the pineapple purée and 1 tablespoon sugar and microwave on HIGH for 2 minutes. Keep aside.
2. In another microwave safe bowl, mix together the milk, water, remaining sugar and saffron and microwave on HIGH for 2 minutes. Keep aside.
3. In another microwave safe bowl, mix together the semolina and ghee and microwave on HIGH for 2 minutes, stirring after every 30 seconds.
4. Add the semolina to the milk mixture and microwave on HIGH for 4 minutes.
5. Add the cooked pineapple, cardamom powder, mix well and serve hot.

SHAHI RABDI

Picture on page 21

Thickened milk flavoured with saffron and cardamom. Making rabdi has never been so easy. The condensed milk helps to thicken the rabdi quickly, while the cottage cheese helps to add body and flavour to the rabdi. It is necessary to use unsalted paneer for this recipe as salted paneer will cause the milk to split.

Preparation time : 5 minutes.   Cooking time : 6 minutes.   Serves 4.
---

1 cup milk
1 cup paneer (cottage cheese), grated
½ cup condensed milk
¼ teaspoon cardamom (elaichi) powder
a few strands saffron
1 teaspoon ghee
a few drops rose essence

For the garnish
1 tablespoon chopped pistachios

1. Mix all the ingredients together in a large microwave safe bowl and microwave on HIGH for 6 minutes.
2. Serve chilled garnished with the chopped pistachios.

Handy tip : Fill the microwave safe bowl to only ¼ its height, leaving enough space for the milk to rise in the microwave, without spilling over.

RICE KHEER

Thick and creamy rice dessert flavoured with fragrant cardamom powder

Preparation time : 5 minutes.   Cooking time : 14 minutes.   Serves 4.

6 tablespoons long grained rice
2 cups milk
¼ cup condensed milk
4 tablespoons sugar
½ teaspoon cornflour mixed in 1 tablespoon milk
few strands of saffron dissolved in 1 tablespoon milk
½ teaspoon cardamom (elaichi) powder

1. Wash and drain the rice.
2. Add 1½ cups of hot water in a Microwave safe bowl along with the rice and microwave on HIGH for 8 minutes.
3. Cover and keep aside for at least 10 minutes.
4. Mash lightly to break the rice grains.
5. Add the milk and microwave on HIGH for 3 minutes.
6. Add the condensed milk and sugar and mix well. Microwave on HIGH for 2 more minutes.
7. Add the cornflour paste, saffron, cardamom powder and microwave on HIGH for 1 more minute.
   Serve warm.

COCONUT BARFI

Grated coconut is cooked to perfection with sugar, milk and ghee to make this all time favourite barfi. Be very careful whilst cooking this dessert as even a few extra seconds can cause the barfi to harden up.

**Preparation time : 10 minutes.   Cooking time : 4 minutes.
Makes 10 pieces.**
---

1 cup fresh coconut, grated
¼ cup milk
3 tablespoons sugar
1 teaspoon cardamom (elaichi) powder
a few drops saffron yellow colour
2 teaspoons ghee

1. In microwave safe bowl, mix together the ghee and fresh coconut and microwave on HIGH for 2 minutes, stirring once after 1 minute.
2. Add the milk, sugar, cardamom powder and yellow colour and microwave on HIGH for 2 minutes, stirring once after 1 minute.
3. Remove and spread the mixture onto a greased thali with a 125 mm. (5") diameter and allow it to set for 1 hour. Cut into rectangles and store in an air-tight container.

DOODHI KHEER

Grated bottle gourd is cooked in a combination of milk and milk powder to make a quick and delicious kheer. You have to squeeze out the excess moisture from the grated bottle gourd and cook it in ghee till it dries up in order to make a creamy kheer.

Preparation time : 10 minutes.   Cooking time : 8 minutes.   Serves 2.

1 cup bottle gourd (doodhi), grated
⅓ cup sugar
½ cup milk powder
1 cup milk
a pinch cardamom (elaichi) powder
1 tablespoon ghee

For the garnish
1 tablespoon slivered almonds

1. Squeeze out all the excess water from the bottle gourd and keep aside.
2. In a bowl, mix together the sugar, milk powder, milk and cardamom powder. Keep aside.
3. In a microwave safe bowl, mix together the ghee and bottle gourd and microwave on HIGH for 3 minutes, stirring once after 2 minutes.
4. Add the milk mixture, mix well and microwave oh HIGH for 5 minutes, stirring once in between after 2½ minutes.
   Serve hot garnished with the slivered almonds.

Handy tip : Fill the microwave safe bowl to only ¼ its height, leaving enough space for the milk to rise in the microwave, without spilling over.

WALNUT BARFI

Gone are the days when one had to slave for hours on the hot stove to make a barfi. This walnut barfi is cooked for only 3 minutes.

**Preparation time : 10 minutes.   Cooking time : 3 minutes.
Makes 6 pieces.**

½ cup walnuts, crushed
2 tablespoons sugar
2 tablespoons milk powder
2 tablespoons milk
a pinch nutmeg (jaiphal) powder
1 teaspoon ghee

1. In a bowl, mix together the sugar, milk powder, milk and nutmeg powder and keep aside.
2. In a microwave safe bowl, mix together the walnuts and ghee and microwave on HIGH for 2 minutes, stirring once after 1 minute.
3. Add the milk mixture, mix well and microwave on HIGH for 1 minute.
4. Remove and spread in a greased 125 mm. (5") tray and allow to set for 1 hour.
5. Cut into diamond shapes and serve

1. PINEAPPLE KESARI, Recipe on page 101
2. BHAPPA DOI, Recipe on page 109

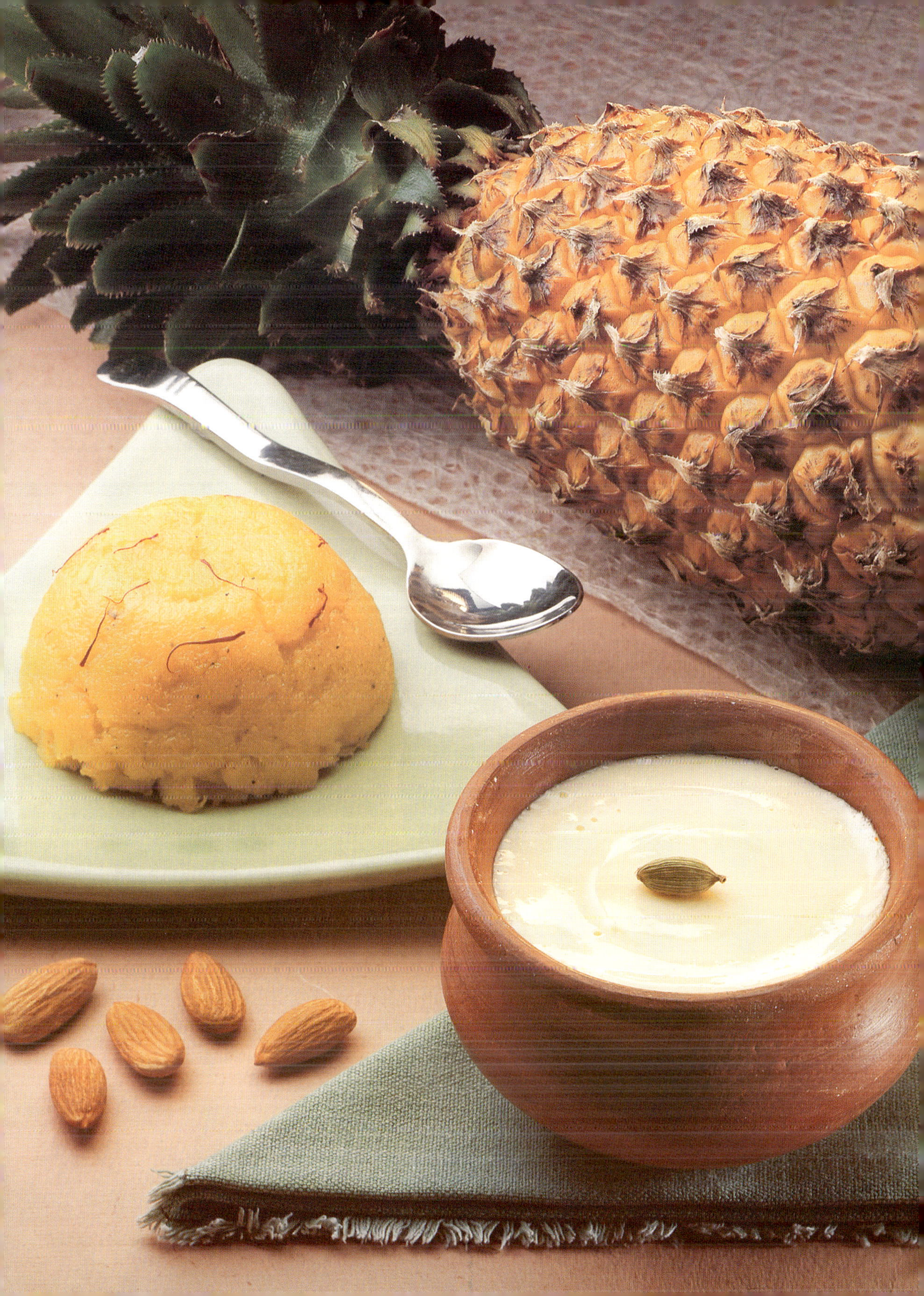

APPLE KHEER

Apple and milk combine with nutmeg and cardamom to make a delicious kheer. The quantity of sugar required will depend on sweetness of the apples. Use sweet juicy apples for best results.

**Preparation time : a few minutes.   Cooking time : 6 minutes.
Makes 2 cups approx.**

---

1 cup apples, peeled and grated
1½ cups full fat milk
2 teaspoons cornflour
2 tablespoons sugar
a pinch nutmeg (jaiphal) powder
¼ teaspoon cardamom (elaichi) powder

1. Combine the apples, milk, cornflour and sugar in a large microwave safe bowl and mix well.
2. Microwave on HIGH for 6 minutes, stirring once after 3 minutes.
3. Add the nutmeg powder, cardamom powder and mix well.
   Serve chilled.

BHAPPA DOI

Picture on page 107

A microwave version of the traditional Bengali "Steamed Sweet Curds".

Preparation time : a few minutes.   Cooking time : 1 minutes.   Makes 4.

1 cup thick curds
1 cup condensed milk

For the garnish
4 whole cardamoms (elaichi)

1. Combine the curds and condensed milk in a bowl and whisk well so that no lumps remain.
2. Pour into 4 earthen ware bowls (approx. 25 ml.) and microwave on HIGH for 1 minute.
3. Allow it to stand for 2 to 3 minutes.
4. Refrigerate and serve chilled garnished with the whole cardamoms.

MAKAI JAJARIA

A Rajasthani corn dessert made in a jiffy. This dessert tastes best when made with fresh corn. However, you may even use the frozen corn kernels when fresh corn is not in season.

Preparation time : 10 minutes.   Cooking time : 8 minutes.   Serves 4.

---

2 nos. sweet corn cobs, grated
1½ cups milk
½ cup sugar
¼ teaspoon cardamom (elaichi) powder
2 tablespoons ghee

For the garnish
4 pistachios, sliced

1. In a microwave safe bowl, add the ghee and grated corn and microwave on HIGH for 2 minutes.
2. Add the milk and microwave on HIGH for 4 minutes.
3. Add the sugar and microwave on HIGH for 2 minutes.
4. Add the cardamom powder, mix well and serve garnished with the sliced pistachios.

GARAM GOLPAPDI

Picture on page 89

This dish is also called sukhadi in some parts of Gujarat. This is a version of Golpapdi, that is served warm and not cut into the traditional diamond shaped cubes.
The trick to making this version is to add the gur after the wheat and ghee mixture has cooled to a comfortable temperature and yet allows the gur to melt and caramalize thus giving it a characteristic crunch. The milk is added to keep the golpapdi in a soft molten stage.

Preparation time : 5 minutes.   Cooking time : 3½ minutes.   Serves 4.

1 cup whole wheat flour (gehun ka atta)
1 teaspoon saunf (fennel seeds)
1 teaspoon khus-khus (poppy seeds)
½ cup grated jaggery (gur)
2-3 tablespoons milk
¼ teaspoon cardamom (elaichi) powder
½ cup ghee

For the garnish
1 teaspoon sliced almonds and pistachios

1. Combine the ghee and the wheat flour in a glass bowl and microwave on HIGH for 3 minutes, stirring after every minute, till it turns golden brown in colour.
2. Add the saunf, khus-khus and microwave for 30 seconds.
3. Remove from the microwave and stir for a few minutes till the mixture cools down slightly.
4. Add the grated jaggery and mix well till it dissolves into the flour mixture.
5. Microwave for a few seconds (approx. 10 seconds) if the jaggery has not melted completely.
6. Add the milk and cardamom and mix well.
   Serve hot garnished with the sliced almonds and pistachios.

Continental Desserts

CHOCOLATE SPONGE CAKE

This basic sponge recipe can be used to make many iced cakes and gateaux or even enjoyed on its own.

The cake may appear to be a little moist and sticky on the surface even after it has been cooked for the time specified, but it is actually cooked. Allow the cake to rest, covered for atleast 10 minutes after removing it from the microwave, as the steam trapped within will continue to cook the cake.

Preparation time : 10 minutes.   Cooking time : 5 minutes.
Makes 1 cake.

½ cup plain flour (maida)
¼ teaspoon soda bi-carb
2 tablespoons sour curds
1 tablespoon cocoa powder
⅓ cup powdered sugar
½ teaspoon vanilla essence
¼ cup melted butter

1. Mix together the curds and soda bi-carb in a bowl and keep aside.
2. Sieve the flour and cocoa powder. Keep aside.
3. Heat ¼ cup of water in a microwave safe bowl on HIGH for 1 minute, add the melted butter and sugar and mix well.
4. Add the flour mixture, curds and vanilla essence and mix lightly to make a smooth batter.
5. Spoon the mixture into a 100 minutes 100 mm. (4") diameter greased, microwave on HIGH for 4 minutes.
6. Remove form the microwave and allow the cake to stand for approx. 10 minutes. Unmould and use as required.

VARIATION : VANILLA SPONGE CAKE

To make vanilla cake simply omit the cocoa powder from the recipe.

CHOCOLATE BROWNIE

A rich, dark chocolate brownie which is ideal for a tea party or even as a dessert if served with a dollop of vanilla ice-cream.

Preparation time : 15 minutes.   Cooking time : 5 minutes.
Makes 1 brownie (8 pieces).
---

1 cup plain flour (maida)
½ teaspoon baking powder
½ teaspoon soda bi-carbonate
2 cups (250 grams) dark chocolate, chopped
½ cup butter, softened
¼ cup castor sugar
¼ cup curds, beaten
1 teaspoon vanilla essence
½ cup walnuts, chopped

Other ingredients
1 teaspoon butter for greasing
grease proof paper for lining

1. Grease and line a 150 mm. (6") diameter shallow, microwave safe bowl and keep aside.
2. Sift together the flour, baking powder and soda bi-carb and keep aside.
3. In a microwave safe bowl, add the chocolate pieces and microwave on HIGH for 1 minute. Remove and stir lightly to get a smooth mixture. Keep aside.
4. In another bowl, add the butter and castor sugar and stir with a wooden spoon till the mixture is soft and creamy.
5. Add the melted chocolate to the butter mixture and mix lightly.
6. Add the curds, vanilla essence, flour mixture and walnuts and mix lightly.

7. Pour the batter into the greased and lined dish and microwave on HIGH for 3 minutes.
8. Reduce the temperature to 70% power and microwave for another 1 minute. Remove and keep aside.

Handy tip : To grease and line is to first grease the bowl with butter or vanaspati and then line with a piece of greaseproof paper.

DOUBLE LAYERED CHOCOLATE TRUFFLE GATEAU

Picture on facing page

An all time favourite. Dark chocolate sponge layered with dark and white chocolate makes an irresistible dessert for al chocolate lovers.

> Preparation time : 15 minutes.   Baking time : 1 minute 45 seconds.
> Makes 1 cake.

1 (150 mm. (6") diameter) chocolate sponge cake, recipe on page 113

For the dark chocolate truffle icing
1 cup (150 grams) dark chocolate, chopped
½ cup (100 grams) cream

For the white chocolate truffle icing
½ cup (75 grams) white chocolate, chopped
¼ cup (50 grams) cream

To be mixed into a soaking syrup
2 tablespoons sugar
¼ cup water
¼ tsp vanilla essence

DOUBLE LAYERED CHOCOLATE TRUFFLE GATEAU,
Recipe above

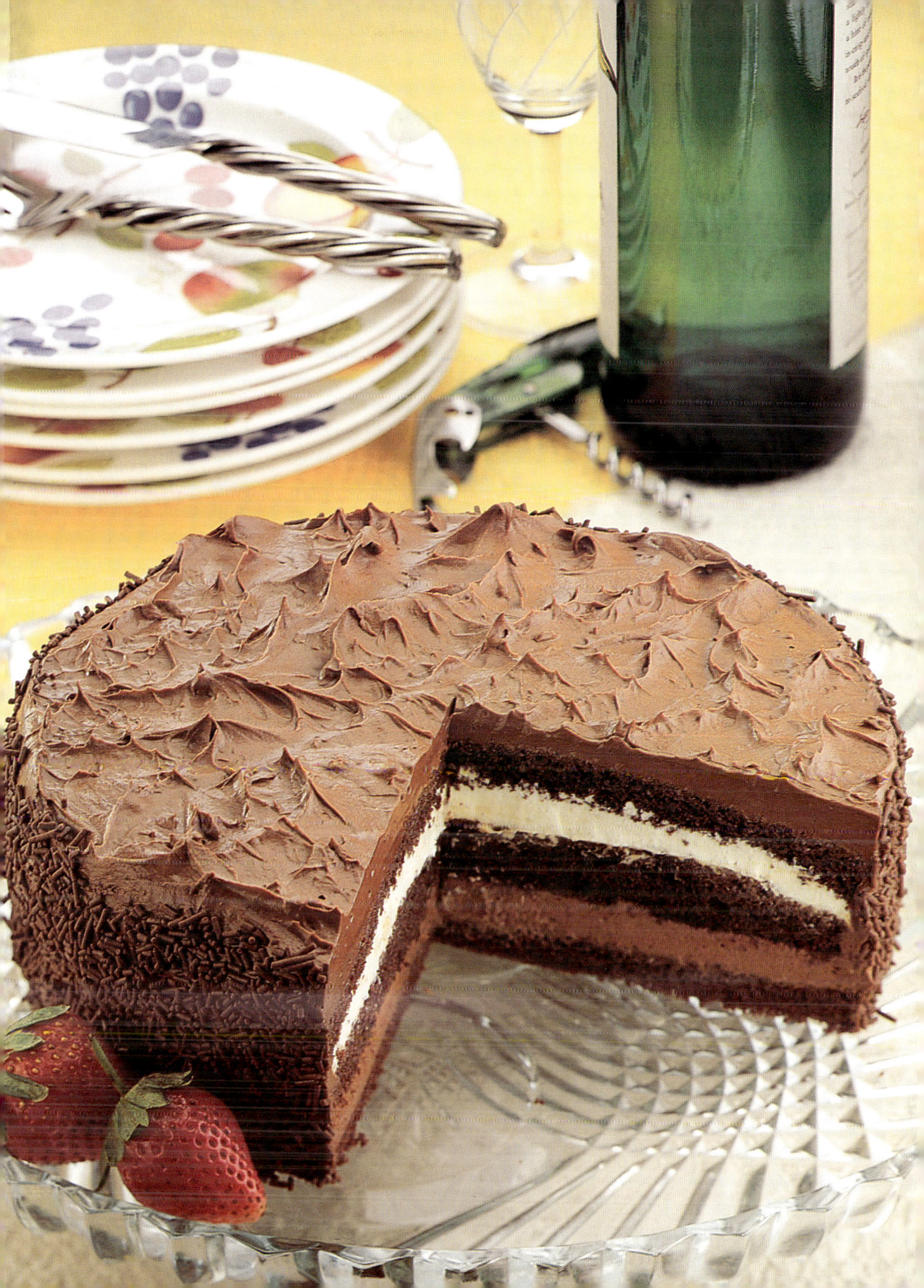

For the dark chocolate truffle icing
1. In a microwave safe bowl add the cream and chocolate and microwave on HIGH for 1 minute.
2. Mix well till there are no lumps and till it resembles a smooth sauce.
3. Stir the truffle over a bowl of ice to cool quickly.

For the white chocolate truffle icing
1. In a microwave safe bowl add the cream and chocolate and microwave on HIGH for 45 seconds.
2. Mix well till it resembles a smooth sauce.
3. Stir the truffle over a bowl of ice to cool quickly.

How to proceed
1. Slice the chocolate cake horizontally into three equal parts.
2. Place one layer of the cake on a serving plate and sprinkle ⅓ of the soaking syrup in order to make the cake moist.
3. Spread half of the dark chocolate truffle icing over the cake layer, sandwich with another layer of the cake.
4. Moisten this cake layer with a little soaking syrup.
5. Spread the white chocolate truffle icing and top of the third cake layer.
6. Moisten this cake layer with the remaining soaking syrup and spread the remaining dark chocolate truffle icing on top and sides.
   Serve chilled.

WHITE CHOCOLATE FUDGE

The gooey chocolate fudge simply melts in your mouth. You may even use dark chocolate for a sinfully delicious variation liquid.
Liquid glucose is available at most stores which stock cooking chocolate and is used to help the fudge to set well and hold shape even at room temperature.

Preparation time : 5 minutes.   Cooking time : 3½ minutes.
Makes 36 pieces.

---

1 cup white chocolate, chopped
¼ cup softened butter
1 cup icing sugar
½ cup fresh cream
¼ cup walnuts, chopped
1 teaspoon liquid glucose

1. Combine all the ingredients except the chocolate in a microwave safe bowl and microwave on HIGH for 2 minutes stirring once after 1 minute.
2. Add the chocolate and microwave on HIGH for 1 more minute.
3. Mix well and microwave on HIGH for 30 more seconds.
4. Pour into a greased 150 mm. (6") square tray.
5. Allow it to set for 4 to 6 hours and cut into 25 mm. (1") squares.
   Serve at room temperature.

DARK CHOCOLATE AND PEANUT BUTTER BITES

Chocolate squares interlaced with peanut butter make yummy after dinner treat. You may also add finely chopped peanuts in addition to the peanut butter for a crunchy variation.

**Preparation time : 5 minutes.   Cooking time : 2½ minutes.
Makes 36 pieces.**

1 cup dark chocolate, chopped
½ cup peanut butter
½ cup condensed milk

1. Combine the chocolate and peanut butter in a microwave safe bowl and microwave for 1 minute stirring once in between.
2. Add the condensed milk and microwave on HIGH for 1½ more minutes, stirring once in between.
3. Pour into a greased 150 mm. (6") square tin and level with the back of a spoon.
4. Allow it to set, cut into 25 mm. (1") pieces and store in an air-tight container.

BREAD AND BUTTER PUDDING

A quick varitaion of the classic bread and butter pudding. You can even use up any left-over slices of bread to make this light and delicious pudding with a lovely muesli and brown sugar crust.

> **Preparation time : 15 minutes.   Cooking time : 2½ minutes.**
> **Serves 4.**

2 slices bread
2 teaspoons butter
2 tablespoons brown sugar
2 tablespoons muesli

To be mixed together for the custard
1 cup milk
1 cup cream
4 tablespoons cornflour
5 tablespoons sugar
¼ teaspoon vanilla essence
2 tablespoons raisins (kismis)

Other ingredients
butter for greasing

1. Apply butter on both sides of the bread slices and cut each slice into 2 diagonally.
2. Grease a 175 mm. x 125 mm. (7" x 5") microwave safe dish and arrange the bread slices on the base of the dish.
3. Sprinkle the meusli on top of the bread slices.
4. Pour the custard mixture gently along the sides of the pan, taking care not to pour the mixture on top of the slices.

5. Sprinkle the brown sugar on top of the bread slices and keep the dish aside for 5 to 10 minutes to allow the bread to soak in the custard.
6. Microwave on HIGH for 2½ minutes. Allow the pudding to hold for 10 to 15 minutes and serve warm.